Béatrice Crawford comes from Paris, is married to an Englishman, lived in California for 17 years, and has lived in Oxford since 1998.

She read German at the Sorbonne. At Stanford University her German MA was on Kafka and her French PhD on Ronsard. She taught 20th century French fiction at Stanford and at Birmingham University Extra Mural Department. Her familiarity with three cultures and languages helps her to look at life from different angles.

Her monologue *'Working Arrangement'* was performed at the 1994 Birmingham Readers and Writers Festival. At the 2003 Oxford Literary Festival, her play, *'Entente Cordiale'*, was long-listed, in the Vodaphone Play Writing Competition.

Voices on the Great Wall - He is still Here has been nearly a decade in gestation. All the events described actually happened. Only people's names have been changed.

Voices on the Great Wall

He is still Here

Béatrice Crawford

To Jane with love

Béatrice

CompletelyNovel Books

Voices on the Great Wall - He is still Here

First published in Great Britain in 2014 by
CompletelyNovel.com

ISBN Number 978 1 849145 55 8

Printed in Great Britain by
Anthony Rowe CPI

In memory of Eric
and for my husband, his father
for our daughter, Isabelle, his sister
for our granddaughters,
Olivia, Chloë, Madeleine, Catriona, Flora, his nieces.

Le vent se lève!… Il faut tenter de vivre!
L'air immense ouvre et referme mon livre,
La vague en poudre ose jaillir des rocs!
Envolez-vous pages tout éblouies!
Paul Valéry. "Le cimetière marin"

There is no Frigate like a Book
To take us Lands away,
Nor any Coursers like a Page
of prancing Poetry -
This Traverse may the poorest take
Without oppress of Toll -
How frugal is the Chariot
That bears a Human soul.
Emily Dickinson

Le vierge, le vivace et le bel aujourd'hui (…)
Stéphane Mallarmé

Pendant quelques minutes, je sentis qu'on peut être près de la
personne qu'on aime, et cependant ne pas l'avoir avec soi.
Marcel Proust. *À la Recherche du Temps Perdu*

CONTENTS

- Prologue -   page 1

Part One HOME

Part Two CHINA

Part Three HOMECOMING

The Jinshanling Great Wall - The YanShan Mountains

A twenty-metre high rampart

B to the fore descending crumbling steps

The Great Wall 长城 Chang Cheng

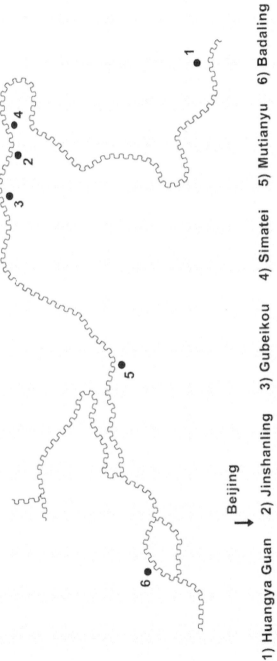

1) Huangya Guan   2) Jinshanling   3) Gubeikou   4) Simatei   5) Mutianyu   6) Badaling

Beijing

Prologue

Let me tell you a story. A true story.

It is the story of B, a Frenchwoman, who goes trekking on the Great Wall of China to raise money for NewShores Children's Hospice.

Why does it come to her one day that she is meant to take up that challenge? At sixty-eight, to go that far, leaving her husband behind for the first time, is rather adventurous. But is it a new chapter in her life, or simply another episode in a journey that started unexpectedly thirteen years ago?

Wherever that journey takes her, the same companions go with her. They are always present, but nowhere to be seen. One of them is ageless, featureless. Some might be tempted to call him God, but B rarely does, and to avoid inadequate metaphors, she calls him the Great Mystery, or GM for short. Like old friends, they challenge each other with serious debates and raging arguments, even sulking silences. The other one is blue-eyed and smiling, with a tall lanky frame. He is her son, Eric, who died thirteen years ago, and is for ever twenty-three years old.

Let us follow their Odyssey. It will take us far away, to the Great Wall. The Chinese call it Chang Cheng, a name resonant, and mysteriously inviting. No more delay. All aboard! Chang Cheng, here we come.

Part One

HOME

1

B signs up

'I'm going to China.'

'Oh...Right...I'm going to take a shower.'

This brief exchange takes place on a dark January morning between B a Frenchwoman and her English husband as they are just waking up. It comes as a surprise for both of them. Why this extraordinary announcement? What has led B to this morning's eccentric decision to go to China? It is as if she has signed some kind of contract during the night with an invisible presence that is now taking control of her life. She has awoken with a feeling of inner peace that she has not known for years. It cannot be put into words, but is very real. Today, it seems to her that where she is in her life is exactly where she ought to be. She needs to understand why this is happening.

Let us go back a couple of weeks. B is sorting brochures piling up on her desk and finds a colourful leaflet inside one of them. Above a picture with mountains and people walking on a path bordered by parapets it says, *Help us to raise money for the NewShores Children's Hospice - Walk 100km on the Great Wall of China - 9 to 19 April.* Of course, it does not concern her, they already support NewShores with regular donations, and she always buys their raffle tickets and Christmas cards. But, she does not throw the leaflet away. It stays on the corner of her desk, catching her eye from time to time.

Over the next few days, the words 'walk' and 'raise money' take an increasing hold on her thoughts. They are like the two faces of a coin that she keeps turning in her mind. She and her husband have enjoyed many walking holidays. For both of them, walking is synonymous with pleasure, but never with raising money. The various fundraising events organised by friends are generally social occasions. She is happy to send a donation, and sometimes to attend them. She admires those involved, and is grateful for never being asked to join them. She has never raised one penny for charity, and has never aspired to.

Now that there is this new and unusual opportunity to take on a personal fundraising challenge, her outlook is changing. She can almost hear the 500 families that NewShores supports appealing to her personally. She feels with them in their personal suffering and is unable to turn away. The growing desire to do something for them will not leave her in peace. Why can she not take the familiar path to her mental hideout, that secluded space she created within herself after the death of her son Eric, that safe retreat where no one can urge her to move on? Even now, years later, in those moments when nothing makes sense any more, she needs a refuge where she can escape reality and lick her wounds.

But this morning, everything has changed. She wakes up, fully aware of the thoughts that have been turning in her subconscious for the last two weeks, since she saw the NewShores brochure. She has now inexorably started her personal journey on the road to the Great Wall. Life has never said its last word until our last day.

At breakfast, the usual practicalities are exchanged between orange juice and muesli.

'Are you going to London by car, or by train?'

'London? It's not Thursday today; it's Wednesday. My committee is on Thursday.'

'Oh... Wednesday?... Is it?...Oh, yes, of course.'

No one mentions China. Who should do it first? Her husband's strategy is always to wait cautiously. He prefers to give her time to prepare her arguments and to present them coherently in the best light. It is safer for both.

At the moment, it suits her. She cannot wait to be alone, free to examine the contradictory thoughts that are swirling in her head. It is no good involving him at this stage. He is a man of instant decision; she is a woman of instant hesitation. Better to bide her time until she can sort things out in her mind and make sense of them. More crucially, when she is conducting her internal debates she prefers him to be out of earshot. It is never done in silence. In her solitary game of questions and answers, when she is assessing her own suggestions, she is ruthless. She comes up with biting retorts to herself, and quite often in a loud voice. The walls are used to hearing her furious arguments. 'How about doing this, rather than that? Are you mad, it would never work!' 'Why not phone them? You must be dreaming!'

Such inner debates are always constructive. She is by herself. No one is given a chance to avoid answering someone else's question, or to accuse the other of not listening. That way, no one comes out of the discussion feeling short-changed or ignored.

This morning, B performs her well-rehearsed ritual of self-assessment, but whichever way she looks at her recent decision she cannot find anything rash or mistaken about it. She emerges with her determination to go to China unshaken. She might have a few aftershocks of self-doubt, and her mind might fill up with reasons to go back on her decision - some people are like that and B is one of them - but this morning she is not even conscious of the danger. She is at Phase Two now. The time for speedy action has come.

When confronted with a new situation, B's first impulse is to make a list of what has to be done. If she is lucky, it may sow the seeds of a strategy in her mind, and grow a variety of useful tactics. What are the key questions? First, how does one take part in a charity challenge? Secondly, how does one raise money? This is all unknown territory for her. Obviously, she must investigate, but without running the risk of appearing totally inexperienced and making a fool of herself. Her courage fails at the prospect, and she seizes the NewShores leaflet on her desk, pressing it against her chest like a talisman. That gesture restores her inner strength, and a quick glance at the leaflet supplies the weapon to fight her dispirited mood. There it is, in black and white, a telephone number preceded by the helpful suggestion, *To find out about this challenge call the NewShores Children's Hospice.* All she needs to do is dial their number and listen.

But she still hesitates, vaguely anticipating a negative answer from them: it is too late; they have closed the admission list; anyway, why would they want to include a sixty-eight-year-old Frenchwoman in their group? 'Stop picturing yourself banging your head against a brick wall,' she tells herself, 'Imagine yourself walking on your own two feet on the Great Wall.' She must choose between these two 'walls'.

It should be mentioned here that B has a habit of building in her head verbal parallels between expressions using the same word in its literal and figurative senses. However far-fetched her plays on words, they are often her best way to stop arguing endlessly with herself. They can provide just the diversion needed to allow her to cease dithering and to move on.

Having to switch constantly from her own language to a foreign one, has made her an incorrigible word juggler, expert at manipulating words and playing private games with them. After her son's death, her ability to juxtapose words, to create unusual symmetries, however contrived, proved unexpectedly to help her. It could bring temporary relief when she needed desperately to re-establish some order in a world that had become out of joint, absurd, where nothing made sense any more. If only temporarily, a new logic would impose itself and help to dispel the confusion in her mind.

One day, when looking for a Bach recording in a music store, she noticed a CD of Vivaldi's Stabat Mater. The sound of the word 'stabat' impelled her to purchase it. She recalled the stabbing pain she had first felt on the day when she was told, 'He is dead', and every day since. While listening to the music, she began to feel part of a community again, the community of the Stabat Mater, of the 'stabbed' mothers. A community where you are entitled to your pain, where you can weep together soothing tears. Over the following days, she brought home more CDs of Stabat Mater, by Pergolesi, Schubert, Rossini. Sometimes, she would simply put them on and wail with them. Some days her attempts at singing with them were more successful.

There is no logic in the death of your child. You have to create your own logic with the few props still available. B. felt it excusable to mistranslate the Latin 'stabat' as 'stabbed'. She was doing it with a purpose. Even if only for a brief moment, that helped her to find her bearings in a world that had lost all meaning; a world in which every minute of every day, wherever she was, the unique reality in her life was the all-invasive presence of absence; a twisted world where only contradictions seemed to rule. Being able to confront that world with her own logic, however twisted, was a sign that her sanity was slowly returning.

One day, when B had the courage again to attend an official dinner party, she found herself sitting next to a man who could not think of a better topic with which to strike up a conversation with a woman, than to question her about her children. Her answer should have been, 'Yes, I have a child,' but it would not pass her lips. She could not adopt a truncated version of the word 'children,' a word that she had enjoyed using for twenty-three years. It seemed to her that to amputate the word's grammatical ending was like denying her son the right to be part of her family, like cancelling his existence. She regained her breath and heard herself whisper, 'Yes, I have two children, but one of them has died.' This total stranger turned out to be not only an old-fashioned gentleman, but also a true human being, articulate and warm-hearted. He did not mumble an embarrassed, 'Oh, I am sorry.' He did not avert his eyes, and turn quickly to the guest on his other side. Generously, he gave B his full attention, encouraged her to talk further, spoke soothing words.

That evening made B aware of the urge within herself to create narrative, to unleash and channel the emotional forces hidden in language, and to use them to create her own fiction. Wrestling with words would be her way to satisfy her longing to rewrite the life that destiny had destroyed, the story that had stopped in the middle of the page, the unfinished story.

This long digression explains why B has to find a weak play on the word 'wall' to remonstrate with herself. She has two options: banging her head against a wall, or putting her feet on the Great Wall; a choice between apathy and action. Creating a shaky parallel between these two sentences makes the choice obvious, and causes her to lift the receiver, dial the NewShores number, and say without hesitation, 'Hello. I am calling about your fundraising challenge on the Great Wall of China. Is it too late to sign up?'

That evening, there is trepidation in B's voice as she rushes to tell her husband about the big step that she has taken. 'I've signed up. Their list wasn't closed.' No time for the homecoming ritual of holding him and his briefcase in her embrace. Depriving him of his daily dose of mutual unflagging devotion is the best way to attract his attention, but what instantly puts him on full alert is to be told that she has done something as concrete and irreversible as signing up. He looks quite anxious now; what has she been up to?

As soon as they are sitting down for dinner, she begins a detailed account of the situation: the NewShores leaflet about the Walk in China that she read by chance; the inner voice that keeps urging her on; her absolute conviction that she is meant to accept the challenge. At this crucial point in her report, she stops talking to glance at him. They are both smiling at each other. His hand slides across the table to grasp hers. Her hand grips his firmly, sending him the comforting message that she is ready to make efforts on her own. So many silent words pass between them in that short pause. After forty-two years of married life, the web they have woven of non-verbal communication is strong.

She has pulled him into her orbit. Now she can safely deploy her lines of argument. Her first intention is to demonstrate that she did not rush headlong into the unknown. The NewShores organiser was charming on the telephone, and sounded efficient and helpful. He had promised to put a package in the post with all the information needed to make a success of this fundraising challenge: terms and conditions, general fact sheet and medical questionnaire. The trekking is no problem. It is no more strenuous than their regular walking holidays. It is only a small section of the Great Wall, a mere hundred kilometres, just a few hundred kilometres north-east of Peking.

She dislikes the word 'Beijing'; it is flat and dull. 'Peking', on the other hand, it sounds like an echo from many thousands of years of Chinese history. It is also what they call it in France and is more exotic. Comparison with the French is intended to give her husband an opportunity to direct a quick-witted counter-attack. No doubt, he will seize that chance to enter the debate safely and on an equal footing. Against all expectations, nothing of the sort happens. He is still listening, and shows no sign of wanting to interrupt her. When she looks at him, slightly puzzled, she recognises a familiar twinkle in his eyes that says, 'It is so good to see you becoming alive and driven again'. She senses that by injecting drama and poetry into the report of her progress with NewShores, she has gained extra respect and credibility. A wave of happiness washes over her as they look at each other and smile.

'How long will you be gone?'

'Oh, only ten days, plus the flights. Don't worry, you won't even have time to miss me,' B replies, having detected concern in his voice.

'Who said I would miss you? I have waited forty-two years for a chance to send you off on your own.'

She couldn't explain why, but his solid and well-timed humour makes her feel comfortably close to him. She sees it as his signal that she can move the conversation to a deeper level. It reassures her that it is the right time to reveal the intimate motives for her recent decision.

But how can she approach that difficult task? Examining together their baggage of shared emotions is by no means rewarding, and they are always reluctant to do it. It is still painful, even thirteen years after Eric's death, and rarely constructive. They see things too differently. She has lived her life in the dock since that loss, wanting the jury to find her as guilty as she feels she is. She has to be her own judge and she will not grant herself bail. Her husband refuses to enter that courtroom. He keeps pleading with her, and encouraging her to rejoin life outside, the life that she is expected to go on living. For everyone's sake she plays the game and wraps herself in the trappings of happiness, but however hard she tries they both know that little exists of her old self except the strength to go on playing the role of wife and mother of their daughter.

There is this sudden decision, all the more revelatory for being so unexpected, this absolute certainty that she is meant to pack and leave for the other side of the world, to aid others in pain like her through raising funds for the NewShores Children's Hospice. The old B is no more. Something has given her the courage and strength to unlock a door and to take her first step outside. Something within her is flapping with eager joy like a sail in the wind.

For a while, neither of them speaks. They are experiencing one of these privileged moments in a couple's life when deeply buried thoughts and feelings invade their minds with such intensity that they have no need to communicate with words. She can read it all in his eyes.

'Do you want me to go?' is all she can say.

'Yes, I really do,' is the emphatic reply to what they both know is a rhetorical question with only one possible answer.

So much has happened today. B feels excited and happy to have contacted NewShores, and to have her husband's warm support. It seems to her that she has been journeying for a long time to the point she has now reached. For the rest of the evening, she is satisfied to let her thoughts wander in a kind of no-man's-land that does not appear on any map. The prospect of walking on the Great Wall of China is still no more real for her than a string of words. She is not even tempted to imagine that journey, or to visualise her exotic destination. No such petty preoccupation as the practicality of finding sponsors for her NewShores trek has yet entered her mind. No doubt, it is already in her husband's practical mind, but he won't destroy the magic of the moment. It is only on the point of falling asleep later that night that she asks dreamily, 'How much do you think I can raise for NewShores?' without expecting an answer.

2

B's appeal

'I think the NewShores information pack has arrived,' announces B's husband the next morning, when examining the post pushed through the letterbox.

'Don't touch it,' she shouts back, rushing downstairs. She wants to experience fully the thrill of discovering what she has committed herself to. Her heart beats fast when she opens the large envelope and spreads its contents out on the dining room table. While reading each page she highlights the paragraphs that need to be re-examined. Soon she finds herself organising them into three groups placed in imaginary pigeonholes: in one pile the forms that require immediate action, like booking an appointment with her GP because she is over sixty; in the next, four pages of suggestions on how to raise money, and the list of what to take with her to China; finally the stack of information from the tour operator organising the Great Wall trekking challenge for charities.

She is so absorbed in her sorting task that she does not hear her husband entering the room until he puts down in front of her a National Geographic issue on China. She looks at him imploringly. He must not say anything before she explains the outline of her plan of action, and her order of priority to achieve it. Pointing at the various papers on the table, she describes the precise timetable that she has in mind. When she stops talking, and glances at him, he says nothing. She reads reflected in his widened eyes the thought that here is a wife who is greatly changed, whose outlook is not as it has been for years, whose appetite for active life has returned. His only role will be to encourage her whenever she wavers in her resolve to pursue her new project. She must be the one in charge.

It is a new sensation for B to feel so committed to supporting NewShores more actively than by a regular contribution. Compared with what the charity needs, the sum she might raise may not be enormous, but it will be useful and she can trust them to spend it wisely. She has kept herself informed on their work, particularly their remarkable achievement of building a second much-needed children's hospice for the region.

The first question on her mind is, 'How does one raise money?' She begins reading avidly the detailed 'A-Z of Fundraising' sent by NewShores. What a shock! Their four pages of suggestions all seem to her to be Herculean tasks. A *'Beer & Skittles'* evening at your local pub - she hates beer, has no local pub, never enters such an establishment; she even needs to consult her English-French dictionary to find out what the word 'skittles' means. A *'Bounce-athon or jump-athon'* - no friends of her age group would, or even could, safely volunteer to join her in such a challenge. A *'Head Shave'* - she would have to hide in a cupboard for months afterwards, and would her thinning hair ever grow back? A *'Parachute jump'* - now, there is an attractive thought, but would it be wise to risk a broken ankle before a 100-kilometre walk on the Great Wall of China? The rest of the list is even less suitable, and she is by now more than ever aware that her relatively sheltered life has not equipped her with the basic skills to become a successful fundraiser.

She has to face the harsh reality. There is only one feasible alternative in her case. She has never used it, and has never wanted to use it. But, like it or not, she has to endure the embarrassment of asking friends and relatives directly whether they would support her Great Wall challenge in aid of NewShores. She must let her conviction that it is for a very worthy cause overcome her scruples. That is what is required from a mother on a mission.

Her first task is to establish a list of potential donors. It is relatively easy to copy names of family from her address book, but a much bigger challenge to make up an extensive list of friends. Where should she draw the line? How should she decide whether she knows them well enough to ask them to support her? She is feeling more and more self-conscious and reluctant to add any more names. Had her husband not encouraged her to include many of the people they meet regularly at official events, she might have given up

It is hard for B, a list maker *par excellence,* to resist the temptation to compile the names and organise them according to her favourite system of colour-coded notes. But this is a serious task that requires her to be adult and methodical. Her beloved computer will prevent her from being lackadaisical or scatterbrained. It will be her trusted helper from now on.

By the end of the day, she has a list of 150 names, and sheets of sticky labels with the mailing addresses of most of them. She places her finished pages in new imaginary pigeonholes on the dining room table. It is not too fanciful to imagine her stepping back to admire her first day's creation and declaring it good.

The next stage is to compose the letter to be sent to those on the list. Although the proposed Great Wall trek can be described in just a few words, B senses that she owes it to her potential supporters to appeal to them more personally. She needs to express persuasively her reasons for taking up the challenge. There will be soul-searching tomorrow. Let us wish her a good night's sleep.

Who would have thought that the following week would be devoted almost entirely to composing that letter? One version after another ends up in the wastepaper basket, and it is already mid-January. How can she justify or even explain her unusual and sudden decision to join the NewShores challenge?

By the beginning of the next week, nagging doubts, hesitations and scruples begin to fade away. The cruellest of all days, 22 January, is approaching. It is as if B's thoughts re-position themselves at the heart of her grief, pinning her down where she was exactly thirteen years ago. Every year, she feels less able to go through that anniversary. If only she could experience again a few minutes of the illusory conviction that it is all a dreadful nightmare, and that she will wake up to find Eric alive. But there have been no such deceptively soothing flashbacks in recent years.

As January darkness descends on the streets and her heart, her desire to embrace the entire cohort of parents pining for their lost children intensifies. How can there be anything more urgent than to support the dedicated professional team at NewShores Hospice? The compulsion that possesses her now overcomes her natural reserve. An inner voice dictates words that translate in an orderly way the flow of raw emotion inside her. She begins to write. Her points and arguments organise themselves convincingly on the page.

22 January

This is the first time I write such a letter. Let me come to the point. A few weeks ago, I received a flyer from the NewShores Children's Hospice : **Walk 100km on the Great Wall of China to help us raise money for NewShores.** *It caught my attention as a personal message to me, and* *soon became an irresistible call. Night after night, I woke up feeling that, if I answered it, for the first time in the thirteen years since our son Eric's death, everything in my life might fall into place again. So I have signed up.*

Here I am, at 68, still enjoying the full use of two working knees that have given me the thrill of climbing rock faces and glaciers in the French Alps, and - for forty years with my husband - the repeated pleasure of walking in California, Wales, Italy, Spain and France. By contrast, when Eric was only sixteen, he took up fencing enthusiastically and in no time became the under-eighteen foil and sabre champion of Southern England. His fencing master judged him a potential Olympic winner. Then, within a year, his knees turned against him, became very stiff and painful. Operations, physiotherapy, nothing helped. His dreams were shattered. No more fencing, also no more tennis, cycling, running and skiing. From then on, for the last six years of his life, he never complained even once about his disabling condition.

My walking 100km on the Great Wall of China will be in memory of Eric, and in celebration of his dignity and immense courage. My French logic has never allowed me to stop asking, 'Why Eric and not me?' So far, I have not found a satisfying answer. I feel that the challenge of the Great Wall offers me for the first time an opportunity to use those sound knees of mine for a better cause than my own enjoyment.

My husband and I, and Eric's sister, Isabelle, have known for thirteen years to the day that when a child dies it's no more 'life goes on' but 'life with pain goes on'. I believe passionately that one way to show real compassion to soon-to-be-bereaved families is to help them to accumulate a capital of happy memories together while there is still time. Such memories never fade away nor die, they are a torch in the darkest hours of despair, they are often the only painkiller on the lonely road ahead. NewShores is a wonderful provider of such happy memories.

It has now two centres helping, free of charge, close to 500 families to make their last months, weeks, days together, free of physical pain and with as much joy and laughter as possible. Their dedication is remarkable, and they are ready to do even more, but only 10% of their funding comes from

19

statutory sources. If you had the generosity to support my 100km walk on the Great Wall, every penny I raised would go to NewShores and allow them to reach more families with a child suffering from a terminal illness. It would help this charity to make the unbearable less unbearable.

If you wish to contribute, please send me a cheque made out to NewShores Children's Hospices Trust which I will forward. It can be gift-aided. Your support will entitle you to a free signed copy of 'Tintin Crawford on the Great Wall', that I shall write after the trek.

I don't intend to fail. I am training for the 100km climb in the YanShan Mountains, up and down the steps of the Great Wall. Having to get out of my sleeping bag in the cold mountain air, without a tap to turn on for a clean hot shower, or a socket to plug in my hairdryer (not to mention having to use the 'long drop' facilities, to quote the trip description), will be the real challenge for me.

I want to thank you for reading this very long letter. As you know, conciseness and British reserve are not my forte. I value your friendship and I feel privileged to be able to share these few thoughts with you. B.

Reading her letter, she knows that she has found words perfectly suited to her purpose. It would be no exaggeration to say that she is possessed now by the joyous exhaustion and pride of a mother holding her newly-delivered offspring. It took courage to compose that letter. She feels grateful to have succeeded.

The next tasks, of typing, photocopying, signing, folding, sealing, addressing, and stamping 150 letters and envelopes, followed by the fastidious counting, checking, and marking of her list, take up the whole day. To her surprise, her husband interrupts her at lunch with a delicious homemade croque-monsieur. She never suspected such cooking talents. Another miraculous achievement on that day.

Late that evening, people could have seen her scuttling through the town clutching close to her chest a bulging plastic bag, and emptying its precious contents into the waiting mouth of a box at the Central Post Office. That night, some unknowing employee ensures that the 150 envelopes are date-stamped 22 January. That night, B falls asleep having spent this anniversary for the first time in thirteen years without shedding a single tear.

The next morning, the excitement of the previous day has died down within B, and given way to a tidal wave of doubts and self-criticism. What had possessed her to write and, worse, to send such a personal letter? How could anyone reading it not feel embarrassed and even annoyed? Why would anyone want to sponsor her, anyway?

To go through the day, she needs to clear her mind of such corrosive thoughts. It is urgent to release the pressure. As soon as her husband appears at breakfast, she rushes through a lengthy list of reasons why she should not have sent her letter. It has become part of their lives that, from time to time, she needs him to listen to her objections to plans that have already been decided and acted upon. His role is to nod absent-mindedly, and to appear to indulge her wavering. It always has an exorcising effect on her mind. However, this morning he interrupts her almost immediately with the curt comment, 'Stop torturing yourself. Just wait and see what happens.' This salutary shock serves to remind her that she must accept the consequences of her decisions concerning the NewShores venture, and keep her dithering to herself. She is the one in charge, and he intends it to remain that way. He is there to provide support only for the positive and rational.

Two days later, among the usual bills and junk mail arrived in the morning, B finds five letters addressed by hand. She opens the first one eagerly, and extracts a letter and a cheque. A quick glance at the cheque takes her breath away. As her brain registers the zeros dancing before her eyes, she hears herself yelling, 'I can't believe it, I can't believe it.' Her screams bring her husband rushing downstairs, ready to provide first aid to a badly injured wife. Instead, he finds himself gazing with her at the evidence, the handwritten figure, '£1,000.'

For a few moments they are both speechless. Eventually, she picks up the accompanying letter and begins to read it aloud. After a few sentences, her voice, choked with emotion, does not allow her to continue, and she hands it over to him. He reads the rest to her while she tries to contain her tears. She cannot believe that so many sympathetic thoughts and enthusiastic comments about her plans could be addressed to her personally. Her heart is bursting with gratitude for such a moving response. Then, rising from deep inside her, comes the familiar insidious thought that she does not deserve such a reward. Is she taking advantage of the situation? Is it not possible to see her new project as self-serving even? There is no merit in her taking up this challenge. She is a fraud.

A flow of negative thoughts invades her until the last ripple has died down. Only then is she able to take stock of the situation. It serves no good purpose to question her motives at every stage. Her tendency to self-deprecation has to stop. She must view it as nothing more than a sign of self-centredness. After what happened over these last few weeks, why can't she accept the role of detached and impassive observer of her life? A life that has been taken over by mysterious forces.

Stiff-upper-lipped well-wishers are bound to see the mental practice of distancing herself from her life as a sign of psychological unbalance, perhaps. But whatever name is given to this distancing process, B has become rather good at practising it. In her case, it is a precious gift that has helped her to find unexpected and providential resilience over the years, despite her grief. How could she have survived the thirteen years since Eric's death without her efforts to believe that it is all happening outside her control, and for reasons that she will be given to understand one day? Such conviction lightens what weighs so heavily upon her.

For as long as she can remember, Bach's music has had that same comforting effect on her, especially certain passages with violin or cello solos. They have been able to transport her to ethereal regions where the air is pure and invigorating, where there is no law of gravity, no crushing feelings. They have the power to open up a new dimension in her mind. They take her to a spiritual world beyond 'too late' and 'never again', beyond joy and suffering, beyond life and death.

This morning, after her initial turmoil of self-doubt, she can look at things from another angle and gain a more rewarding perspective. There is no need to persuade prospective donors that her motives are unselfish. Her duty is to make them feel and understand through her words that her only purpose is to celebrate the real hero of her story, her son Eric. He is the unsung hero of the unfinished story to which her NewShores challenge will add a new page. She also wants to proclaim that, in the end, all of the characters in that story are in the hands of an invisible but ever-present stage director, GM, the Great Mystery.

She has at last reached a constructive phase, where she can accept and welcome without embarrassment every generous donation and every supportive letter. They fill her with joy and immense gratitude to the sender, and indirectly to Eric, who is blowing a strong wind into her sails, and to GM who must be behind it all. There will be more tears, but tears of unmitigated joy, when, by the end of the week, thirty-five more handwritten envelopes drop into her letterbox, all containing generous cheques and beautiful letters. When she arrives at Heathrow two months later, she will have received a staggering total of 115 such letters. Her sponsors will allow her to leave for China having already brought to NewShores £17,000. The following months will add to this sum.

Independently of whether they are large or small, B feels unbounded gratitude for each and every donation received. Her first duty is to handle methodically and scrupulously all of the cheques passing through her hands on their way to NewShores. It becomes part of her daily routine to write down what happens to them at every stage, to pursue a rigorous bookkeeping system until she is sure that they have arrived safely in the Trust account. She adds up, counts and re-counts, checks and double-checks every column on her list of names; again and again. This consuming task continues even into her dreams. If her husband could see behind her eyelids, he would observe the frantic pace of her rapid eye movements, a sure sign of intense cerebral activity.

Her generous sponsors emerge vividly from the sea of figures. She can imagine them writing their moving letters to express thoughts that they would never say to her directly. Many a line is blurred on the page by her tears as she reads them.

One friend, who responds generously to her appeal, cannot resist teasing her with his anti-European sense of humour. He sponsors her per mile, up to the announced length of 100km, with a cheque for £62.13. Then there is the large envelope received from her daughter in Scotland. Added to her own cheque, are several more contributed spontaneously by colleagues at the GP practice where she works. As mothers of young children, a few of them had shed tears while reading her January letter. The thought of children dying had touched a sensitive chord.

And then comes the incredible offer of one half of an entire personal fortune! Her seven-year-old granddaughter calls from Scotland.

'Grand-Maman, when you go on the Great Wall, can I sponsor you?'

'Oh, darling, how sweet of you, but…'

'I'll give you £1.'

'Oh, darling, thank you. You are so kind, but it's too much. You must keep it to buy something for yourself.'

'Oh, no, Grand-Maman. I've another pound from the Tooth Fairy. I've lost two teeth.'

She hangs up knowing that she will for ever remember this conversation.

In these last few weeks, many joys have come to B, directly or indirectly, through Eric's life. They are precious gifts to be stored in her personal treasure chest. They will never lose their sparkle.

3

B's trek preparation

For months, the dining room table is B's headquarters. Letters from donors fill a large box, various items of correspondence with NewShores pile up in their respective trays, not much empty surface is left. Her husband never complains, and eats his meals hunched over a small coffee table. He is plainly delighted to discover a wife who sees at last the advantage of being methodical and well organised.

The part she relishes most is writing to her friendly supporters. Since they evidently believe in her, she ought not to disappoint them. They deserve to be thanked for their generosity. Her expressions of gratitude cover the entire A4 page of her thank-you letters. Before she leaves, another card will inform them that she is training seriously for this challenge, and that she will tell them afterwards how she coped with it. By the time she returns safely from China and resumes home life, her 115 supporters will each have received three exuberant messages from her. Did they find the time to read them all to the last line? We shall never know, but her conscience is clear.

There is more than one way to look at one's actions in life. The French writer La Rochefoucauld contended in his *Maximes*, that, however noble our behaviour appears to be, deep down it is selfishness that motivates us. At her Lycée in Paris, years ago, B read his book and agreed with most of it. Some of his maxims still echo in her memory. Could it be that his pessimistic and self-deprecatory views of human nature have marked her? Is that why she often suspects that her desire to keep her donors regularly informed of her progress is nothing more than an excuse for self-promotion? Or could her logorrhoea reflect a need to drown her self-doubts?

But such a frame of mind has a paralysing effect, and she must fight it. Laughing at her preposterous tendency towards navel-gazing is the only way for her to move on. Her sense of humour is a trusted old friend; it has always helped her to get the better of her self-criticism. Why does she not give free rein to her imagination? Why not make her letters look appealing, and amusing, so that no one will mind receiving three more of them, or worse suspect her of hidden motives? She is ready to concentrate her efforts on the task ahead. No more hesitation.

Each letter is going to be on one sheet of paper folded in two, with a funny picture on the front and the correspondence on the other side. At the front of her thank-you letter, she puts a picture of a little old lady with a handbag, wearing a boater and zooming along on a mini-scooter. Below it says, 'Chang Cheng here we come', followed by her personal message. Perfect coordination between the typist, the computer and the printer is difficult to achieve. B's wastebasket soon overflows with crumpled pages, some with the text printed upside down, or overlapping the picture, some on the wrong side of the page.

Eventually she produces a perfect copy by pure luck, she has not the faintest idea how or why.

Fortunately, the practical aspects of the NewShores challenge do not pose such insoluble problems. Clear guidelines are provided by the tour company, telling B what to do for the medical check-up, the immunisations, the passport and visa. Their list of what to take in her luggage is straightforward for a veteran walker, except for two items, toilet rolls and a cigarette lighter. In small Chinese villages, the first is still a luxury and practically non-existent, but she is at a loss to divine the use of the lighter. It will be needed during the trek to burn any piece of that paper that she might otherwise leave behind. Needless to say, she decides to delete it from her list. She is not keen to set China on fire, but above all she would rather not think of the terrifying prospect of having to answer a call of nature while trekking on the bare Great Wall with a group of British walkers. For her, that is by far the most challenging feature of the whole adventure.

Three weeks before the departure date, a dinner organised by NewShores at a local pub gives her a chance to meet most of the other volunteers. They are of all ages and sizes, and it turns out that she is the oldest of the group. Apart from one tall man younger than her by one year, the others are in their prime. Soon, a few of them compare notes about their most imaginative ways to raise funds, for example standing at Tesco's door dressed as a clown and shaking a collection box. Her heart fills once more with gratitude to her generous sponsors who have saved her from such an ordeal. When others exchange useful advice, based on their experience of a charity trek in the Andes the previous year, it makes her wonder whether she is out of her depth and very presumptuous to join such a competent group.

Nobody smokes at that dinner, but she cannot resist enquiring about reactions to the requested cigarette lighter. No other topic, it seems, could have launched a more animated general conversation. It works like magic to create an *esprit de corps* within the group. All at once, everyone is competing to discuss, with graphic details and *risqué* anecdotes, the various ways in which this item could be put to good use during the walk on the Wall. The rest of the evening is much more relaxed and convivial, and she returns home feeling comfortable about eleven days in their company.

After two months of planning and dedicated effort, B should be allowed to enjoy peace of mind and a few hours of well-deserved day-dreaming before flying off to China. But life is full of incongruity. It has a plethora of tricks to keep us on our toes. B is not meant to feel carefree yet. She finds herself, through no fault of her own, on a roller coaster. The strange and unexpected episodes that punctuate this short period are well worth telling..

To boost her confidence, many of her friends are eager to tell her about their Chinese experiences and to emphasize how 'frightfully steep', and 'abominably slippery when wet', and 'dreadfully hazardous and exhausting', it is to walk on that Chinese construction. Perversely, these horror stories have the immediate effect of reviving B's old mountaineer's spirit, and of rekindling the enthusiasm of her climbing youth, when the sign 'Danger Zone' attracted her like a magnet.

Come what may, she knows she can trust her sense of balance, and her old but newly-resoled walking boots that will adhere to any surface. Nothing can shake her faith in her invulnerability, even when she comes face to face with the first casualty case returning from China. It is a friend with a skateboard-like contraption strapped to her left leg, bent at the knee, to support her ankle encased in plaster. What has happened? She had recently stood at the bottom of the Great Wall, looking up at it in awe. As she swivelled to go through the turnstile leading to the first ascending steps, her reluctant Achilles tendon had snapped.

Nothing of the sort could happen to B. For a woman of 68, she is very fit. Getting her doctor's authority to take up the Great Wall challenge is a pure formality. He puts his seal of approval at the bottom of the official form. Neither of them has any reason to expect her to come back to the surgery until her winter flu vaccination is due.

Who would have thought that only a fortnight before departure she would be limping with severe pains in her left foot, in need of urgent medical attention? She finds herself back in the surgery showing a red and hot swollen ankle that hurts night and day. An unfamiliar woman doctor takes a quick look at it, touches it lightly with the back of her hand, and declares, 'You have got cellulitis, and....' 'Certainly not,' interrupts B, who cannot believe that she is hearing such an asinine diagnosis. Just because she is French, she is being accused of having *cellulite*. Even worse, it is a woman who dares to accuse her. Whoever has heard of *cellulite* on the ankles?

'I can assure you that you are showing all the symptoms of cellulitis. But antibiotics will get rid of it in a few days.'

'Antibiotics? I can't see why,' exclaims B, more and more convinced that the many Britons who prefer to be treated in France are justifiably prejudiced against such ignorant doctors.

'Well, let me go and ask for a second opinion,' concedes at last the frustrated doctor, as she escapes from the consulting room. Seconds later, she returns with a fresh-faced junior doctor who repeats the same diagnosis in a deep and self-assured voice. B limps out of the surgery, clutching a prescription for antibiotics that she has no intention of taking.

Driving back home, she fulminates at the wheel, alternately shrugging her shoulders and banging her forehead with the palm of her hand. Other drivers must be wondering what drugs she is on. When she tells her husband that she wants to tear up the prescription, he insists that he will get it filled for her.

As soon as he is gone, she rushes to her computer to look up the word 'cellulitis', to obtain solid proof of the doctor's poor judgement. What a shock to discover that it has nothing to do with the dreaded '*cellulite*' that every French woman of a certain age fears discovering on her thighs. Cellulitis is a well-documented infection, and her ankle indeed presents all of its symptoms. Now, the redness and heat of her left ankle has risen to her face as well. How could she behave so badly with this poor doctor? Why did she, once again, mishear, misunderstand and misuse the English language, and jump to the wrong conclusion? Now she is only too eager to swallow those competently prescribed antibiotics. Within days she is pain-free and no longer limping.

When the problem reappears a week later, she sees the same doctor again, for a repeat prescription. After a flurry of apologies, she explains the linguistic reasons for her misbehaviour. Anybody entering the consulting room would have found two women wiping tears of laughter from their cheeks. She will learn later that this episode with a hysterical French patient has become one of the favourite stories at the medical group's meetings whenever general hilarity is needed.

In just a week, she will be flying to China. None of these mishaps has lowered B's spirit. What else could go wrong? Nothing? Absolutely nothing. All that is left to do is to pack her bag. First, following the advice of a friend's friend who has been on the same Great Wall challenge, she must buy a silk sleeping bag liner. The sheets provided during the trip will often have been slept in a few times already. She finds the last one available in the sports shop, a very elegant liner in black silk. But when she tries to insert herself into its mummy-like shape, while lying on her bed at home, disaster strikes. The seam on the already frayed side opens up over more than half its length. It takes her more than half a day, driving to specialist outdoor shops, until she finds another one. As a precaution, before buying it, she tests it by lying inside it on the dusty floor, at the feet of the young sales assistant who is laughing uncontrollably. Her dedication pays off. She is now the proud owner of a generously-cut, securely-stitched, midnight-blue, top-of-the-range silk liner that weighs only a few grams. In the weeks to come it will prove an invaluable purchase.

Today, on 9 April, she must leave for Heathrow within a few hours. Why does she look so stressed? She should have been resting with a clear conscience. But she has hardly slept, Many times in the night she has got up to open, unpack, repack and close her suitcase. Either exchanging a pair of thick socks for two pairs of thin ones, or replacing a V-neck jumper by a buttoned cardigan, or adding a second toilet roll and a bigger pack of Johnson's baby wipes. She is drenched in perspiration at the thought that in a few hours, whatever she has chosen to put in her suitcase is going to be all that will be available to her for eleven whole days in China. She grabs her suitcase, spreads the entire contents on the bed, and grimaces. After a vigorous session of head-scratching and nose-rubbing, she throws everything back into the suitcase, closes it violently and leaves the room holding it at arm's length to give it hurriedly to her husband already at the front door.

'Let's go', she orders.

'Are you sure you have got everything you need for the trip?'

'In all probability, I have not and you know that as well as I do, so why do you ask?'

That morning, her husband's talent for defusing B's explosive moods is put to the test. What would work best? Wordy explanations or complete silence? He decides to remain neutral and detached, and to concentrate on driving fast to Heathrow.

4

B's adventures begin

Locking the front door, driving away, adding mile upon mile between home and her destination always has a calming effect on B. As she settles down in the car taking her to the airport, purely as a precaution, she takes a few deep breaths and exhales, counting to ten slowly to keep herself relaxed. She is soon rummaging in her small travel bag. Is her passport there? Has she removed her bank card and left it in a drawer at home, having decided at the last minute that no one would accept it on the Great Wall? But her face shows no sign of anxiety while she performs this traditional ritual. By the time they are on the motorway, she is exchanging jokes with her husband. Wrapped in her anorak and rugged trousers, her feet in walking boots, she feels light and ready to float away, far away.

The approach to a major airport has something surreal about it. It looks like a different country already. The grey amalgam of houses on each side of the road flattens gradually to be absorbed into the earth's surface. The sky invades this emptiness, inviting you to jettison ballast and take to the air. B's feet hardly touch the pavement when she steps out of the car and walks towards Heathrow's Terminal C. How appropriate this word, 'terminal'. Something inside her comes to an end, when she enters the building and the automatic door closes behind her. What exactly, she could not say, but she feels exhilarated and reassured. From now on, activity on *terra firma* is of no importance for her. She has cut her moorings and is ready to sail away on her voyage of discovery towards unfathomable adventures.

Her husband can hardly keep pace with her as she hurries along the line of check-in desks. Suddenly she turns towards him.

'I can see them. They are all here. Let me carry my suitcase. I'll say "goodbye" now.'

'Oh, don't worry, I'll come with you.'

'But there is no need.'

'What do you mean, there is no need?'

What goes through B's mind right now is not far from early memories of the embarrassing times when her mother would hug her at the entrance door of the Lycée on the first day of school. But, on second thoughts, should she not show more maturity today, over half a century later, and rejoice at having someone who cares for her? Ageing should teach us to appreciate and to cherish our mixed emotions in the light of past experiences.

When she joins the NewShores group waiting at the far end of the terminal, she announces cheerfully, 'This is my husband. He wants to make sure that it's safe to let me spend eleven days alone with you lot!' Nobody laughs and her husband looks ill at ease. 'You lot'. He has never heard B use such an expression. Her inappropriate familiarity sends him the signal that it is time for him to leave her to deal with the situation, and to endure alone the consequences of her behaviour. After shaking everybody's hands hastily, and distributing good wishes for the trip, he pulls B to the side for a quick embrace and walks away.

By now the group has fragmented into smaller groups already engaged in animated conversations. B stays at the side unwilling to make the effort to join in. She is the odd one out and does not mind. She often finds herself stranded on the lonely river bank that no one can reach without swimming across the stream into which grieving parents are plunged. A familiar feeling for her, although not as unpleasant or even as painful as it used to be. It has not diminished over the years, but her strategy to make it manageable has improved. It implies retreating within herself, of course, and makes her unwelcome in groups. Already she knows that this NewShores group expects everyone to show true team spirit. How will they accept that she is there for her own personal challenge, a challenge that sets her apart?

Emma, the Trekkers World tour leader standing in the middle of the group, calls for silence from everyone on the printed list that she is holding. Their names are all on her airline group ticket. She must show it at every gate, and have them checked and counted. It is a lengthy process and it would help if they could remember in which order she is calling them. Everybody is paying attention now, eager to go through the essential formalities of checking in, going through security, and finding the gate for their Aeroflot flight, as quickly as possible.

At last they all arrive at the correct gate and can see through the large bay windows of the waiting area, the Aeroflot plane for their flight to Moscow. A few trapdoors under its belly are wide open, and a couple of technicians are tapping and twisting parts of the engine. After a while a voice announces, 'We are sorry for the delay and will be calling you soon.'

Two hours later the same voice declares, 'Unfortunately the plane needs more investigation and the flight is now cancelled.' Emma gathers everyone around her and explains that the next flight to Moscow leaves in six hours. It means they would have to wait five hours in the middle of the night in the transit area in Moscow airport before a plane takes off for Beijing. The only sensible thing to do is to delay their departure by a day.

And that is how the first night of that NewShores challenge was spent in a Best Western Motel fifteen miles away from Heathrow. In the morning, the dedicated volunteers queue up at the Aeroflot desk and receive as a gesture of good will from that airline a voucher for a free ticket to be used later at their convenience. Everyone in the group tears their voucher into small pieces and scatters them on the counter as a gesture of 'who-would-want-to-travel-with-you?'.

At last, they find themselves sitting in the plane. Jokes are exchanged, not so much to dissipate hidden feelings of unease as to express the joy of having overcome adversity.

'Are we sure that all the missing nuts and bolts have been replaced?'

'Did they have the right spanners?'

'How many cans of WD40 have they used on the rusty parts?'

Only B remains silent in her seat. Why is she not enjoying the moment? Why can she not at least pretend enjoyment? Why is she fighting tears? She sees in her mind's eye Eric sitting, like her, in the plane that took him away for his year out to work in a poor kibbutz. If only she could fall asleep soon, as she is generally able to do during flights, it would be a relief.

While the aircraft takes off and begins its ascent, she settles down as comfortably as she can in her aisle seat and closes her eyes. Suddenly, one of the overhead lockers bursts open and a big cardboard box falls heavily with one of its edges hitting the head of the passenger below. Who is the unfortunate victim? Of the three hundred passengers on that plane, why does it have to be B? She is immediately surrounded by cabin crew and a few passengers.

Among them, is a young man who had joined the NewShores group at Heathrow, who asks her, 'Are you all right? I am Jimmy, your GP.' B remembers having read in the Trekkers World brochure that they always provide a team with one tour leader and one doctor. 'Oh, Hi, I'm fine, don't worry. I don't break easily, lucky me that these vodka bottles didn't break either.'

The incident has cheered her up. Being on a roller-coaster ride full of unexpected episodes that all deserve to be told one day, is that not what she secretly hopes to happen on this trip? Already, before it has even started, this NewShores fundraising challenge provides her with an exciting narrative. She feels privileged now and soon falls into peaceful sleep.

On arrival in Moscow, the group is corralled in a plate-glass enclosure with locked sliding doors in the dingy transit area of the airport. As a born rebel, B cannot stand it for very long and attempts to open them. The stern rebuke she receives from the unsmiling customs officer watching them from behind the glass door of that cage reminds her that she is on Soviet territory. He could be from the KGB. Four hours later, he takes them into the next glass cage where they must remove shoes, socks and several layers of clothing, before walking through the body scanner. When they are finally released into the departure section, a few of them hurry along the deserted corridors in need of comfort breaks, while the others run in every direction in search of something to drink.

Let us join them five hours later when they are all again in the air on the second leg of their flight. B will never know why, but when she steps into the plane the air stewardess directs her to the first-class section, and invites her to sit in one of its wide seats at the front with plenty of space to stretch her legs. As soon as the seatbelt sign has been switched off, a flight attendant adjusts the back of her seat to a reclining position, pulls out a footrest, and puts a blanket over her. A quick look around shows her that only two other NewShores volunteers are in that section. But why wonder how she deserves such an unexplained privilege when all she desperately wants to do is to fall asleep? And so she does, in the lap of luxury.

A gentle tap on her shoulder startles her out of a deep sleep. What's happening? Where is she? Whose face is it smiling above her? What is he saying? 'Would you like to have your breakfast?' Breakfast? Now? She tries to gather her wits together. Is food the best way to fight jet lag? Should she wait until later? Raising the back of her seat, she struggles to a half-sitting position. 'Breakfast? What time is it?' The Aeroflot steward's reply seems to her still-sleepy mind to be a question with something about Moscow in it. A wave of panic washes over her and she shrieks, 'Oh no! I am not going to Moscow, I am going to Beijing!' The steward bends down to her level, and pats her on the forearm, 'We are all going to Beijing, Madam.'

A few moments later, sitting in front of a plate of smoked salmon and caviar, accompanied by a glass of Champagne, B is satisfied with her lot and ready to enjoy these few hours of flight in first-class. As soon as she takes her first sip, the earlier scene replays on the screen of her mind and she hears what he had actually asked, 'Do you mean local time or Moscow time, Madam?' and she bursts out laughing into her champagne. There is enough wine left to send her oscillating contentedly back and forth between somnolence and daydreaming until the plane glides to a stop on Chinese tarmac.

After some fifteen hours in the air, or in airport transit zones, it is a relief for the flow of bodies and their hand luggage to be disgorged down the wobbly metal stairs of the Tupolev. For B, the welcome sensation of standing fully erect on the ground is quickly changing into a feeling of unexpected elation. Her feet set firmly on Chinese soil for the first time in her life are sending her the message, 'You have touched base, this is Beijing, this is China, it really starts now.' What this mysterious 'it' encompasses she will only discover during the next ten days, and even more profoundly in the years following her return home.

Beijing's brand new airport terminal is huge, futuristic, and nearly empty. It is more the décor for a surrealistic film ready to be invaded by crowds of extraterrestrials than the official building to gain entrance to a capital city with over thirteen million inhabitants. The subdued and silent NewShores group scuttles behind its leader, Emma, along one huge cavernous hallway after another, some covered on each side with colourful panels advertising riches that look disconcertingly western. Could their long march through that gigantic construction become as humiliating as passing through the Caudine Forks had been for the Roman armies?

Earlier, on the plane, they had exchanged stories about their adventures with the unsmiling officials of the Chinese Consulate in London. Extracting the vital entrance visa from them had been no easy task. The first time, B was forbidden to pass through the Consulate doors as her name was not on the list to be admitted for consideration that day. She had not gone properly to 'step 4' when registering on the website, so she did not exist. The second time, she was duly pushed inside the room with fifty other supplicants to stand in a queue for almost two hours. She eventually reached the official desk and was able to shove through the slot at the bottom of a misty glass partition her carefully filled-up four-page application form with a photo attached, and her French passport.

As she had feared, there was to be an immediate hurdle to negotiate successfully. On all French official papers a French female, single or not, keeps for life the family name given at birth by her parents, exactly like all French males; there is gender equality in France, at least on paper. On a passport, the family name of the husband is added to the personal name with the abbreviation '*ép*' meaning '*épouse*'. Her name is followed by the mention, 'ép So-and-so'. As requested, B had reproduced on the form exactly what appeared on her French passport. Alas, the Chinese Cerberus having to decipher a form filled with three surnames, and a forename also in three parts, became suspicious. 'Six names? It's too many!' he said. 'This is the French way; nothing to do with me personally,' she replied vehemently. The employee got up and disappeared as through a trap, taking away the precious pack of documents. By now the external face of the glass partition was getting misty too as B's breathing against it was accelerating. Eventually, he came back and began to scribble on a small form that a visa would be ready within a few days for someone called '*Béatrice,M.,J So-and-So ép Crawford*'. The price to pay for a valid visa was to have to fit the twenty characters of her assigned name on every small slip to be filled in in China.

Let us go back to the airport now. To expedite the passage through the first gate, Emma arranges the fourteen volunteers in the same order as their names appear on the group visa to be handed over, examined and double-checked at every desk or gate. By the third gate, they have all become expert at filling in forms, presenting passports opened at the right page, nodding and smiling gratefully. Each time, B's passage takes a bit longer. Twenty letters, remember! After that, there is nothing to prevent them from reaching a huge hall with a long row of brand new carousels, all immobile except the one at the end. Oh delight, their rucksacks, holdalls and suitcases are already there enjoying a few rides on the luggage roundabout while waiting for them.

There is trepidation in the group as the last automatic doors slide open to reveal the great arrival hall. It is as crowded as arrival halls usually are, but they are immediately accosted by a smiling young Chinese man, his head crowned with an American-style twisted red bandana. Seeing Emma holding a pack of official documents, he rushes up to her, grabs her hand and shakes it excitedly, 'You are Emma? I am Alan, your Chinese tour leader.' Everyone is so sleepy by now that it is only Emma who knows that it has taken months of anxious e-mail exchanges among tour operators based in London, Hong Kong and Beijing to reach these few blessed words, spoken at the right place and at the right time. So many things can go wrong when you have to trust long-distance planning with foreign agencies based in countries on the other side of the world, and not even used to your alphabet.

Alan seems truly happy to see them. He explains that Alan is his tourist guide name for the Westerners, because his Chinese name is too difficult for them to pronounce. He welcomes each member of the group with a vigorous handshake and invites them to follow him to the huge car park just outside the building. To B's astonishment, there are no packhorses waiting outside to be loaded with their bags, and there is no Great Wall to be seen anywhere on the horizon. Instead, in front of her an ultra-modern coach sparkling in the sunshine opens its doors. A man jumps out and starts loading the entrails of his mechanical beast with their luggage. Reassuringly, he looks as Chinese as the tour leader and does not speak English.

Until now, B's notions of China have always been vague and colourless; a few clichéd images collected from odd references in books, or biased and misinformed media. Quite deliberately, she has made no effort to improve them in preparation for this Great Wall charity walk. It would have spoiled everything for her if she had assumed the role of tourist, eager to discover a new country. She is going exclusively as Eric's mother, wanting to celebrate her son's life through this Great Wall trek. She has no other motive.

She has, of course, imagined what it would be like to arrive in a legendary city such as Peking. In her mind's eye, there would be a caravan of horses and an army of tiny Chinese, bowing to her and loading her backpack onto the horses. Instead, she finds at the very beginning of her great adventure that the oriental caravan of her dreams has turned into the pumpkin of a twenty-first-century occidental coach.

Part Two

CHINA

5

The Huangyaguan Great Wall - East

There is complete silence on the coach carrying the fourteen NewShores volunteers. Alan's attempt to give them a full tour briefing to explain how the trip will run, and to give a general plan of events with details of the day ahead, has been wasted. They are all sleeping profoundly. Nothing to do but to let them rest and recover from their long journey. He returns the microphone to the dashboard.

Some two hours later the coach comes to a bumpy stop. It is the perfect wake-up call to bring everybody back to the world of the living. They have arrived at their destination. Actually, not at their first, but at their second destination. Remember, it is not Day One of the organised trip, but Day Two. Thanks to the Aeroflot plane stranded at Heathrow, there was no first night in a comfortable hotel in Beijing as initially planned. Instead, they have skipped directly to the second day of the scheduled trip. The logic of the package booked is implacable.

Before they leave the coach, the dutiful Alan, keen to act in his capacity of official tour leader, grabs the microphone. He explains that they have arrived at Huangya Guan, a village in the heart of the YanShan mountains. Its name means 'yellow cliff pass', alluding to the colour of its spring flowers and its rocks at sunset. It is famous for its ancient fortress built like a labyrinth bounded by hundred-metre long walls. It plugs the gap between sections of the Great Wall built along ridges on either side of this narrow valley, and so offered in the past protection from northern nomads. Today it serves as a guest house where they will spend their first night in China.

Refreshed by a two-hour nap, everyone rushes out of the coach and scrambles to extract bags and suitcases from the luggage bay. They find themselves on a large empty space along a dry river bed. Ranges of craggy mountains tower above them. Before them stands a tall and forbidding façade with large red ceramic Chinese characters running along its crenellated upper edge. As if floating above it, a small platform with wooden pillars supports a curved roof with ornate eaves that rise at the corners. The façade is part of a thick wall that runs for a few hundred metres to left and right, and encloses the whole structure of the fortress. An arched opening without a door is cut like a gaping mouth at the base of the façade.

A shining plaque on the wall announces in Latin characters 'Tianjin Huangya Mountainvilla Guesthouse'. The word 'guest' immediately conjures up in B's mind the kind of oriental welcome she experienced years ago in Japan. She had arrived with her husband at a small mountain village where they had booked a night in a traditional ryokan. There they were greeted by the owner's whole family and staff standing at the door, bowing, smiling and repeating a few friendly and welcoming Japanese words. It was impossible to respond to them in a grateful way other than with some silent gesticulation that they hoped would convey the right message.

But here there is nobody to kowtow to her, nor to welcome her with a smile. Nevertheless, she experiences the feeling of a genuine Chinese welcome. It takes her only a few seconds to realise why. Out of the corner of her eye, she has spotted bright red paper lanterns hanging like plump pumpkins from the lonely tree next to the entrance, and swinging gaily in the light breeze.

She can see even more red lanterns attached to a curved crossbeam in the alley beyond the entrance. They create a blazing contrast with the grey stones and soften the impact of the severe façade. They are a cheerful and heartfelt invitation to come inside.

Lower down, two big stone lions sitting on low plinths on either side of the arched entrance, face the arriving guests. B. is at once charmed and intrigued by these two fierce-looking Chinese beasts posing as inoffensive pet dogs. In a few days, after seeing that same pair in front of every building, be they hotels or private dwellings, she will be tempted to think of them as the Chinese equivalent of British garden gnomes. It is only on her last day in China, when confronted by the seven-metre tall marble lions poised imposingly on their stone plinths for more than five centuries at the entrance to the Forbidden City, that she will again be truly impressed. Fortunately, Alan is always there to provide clear and interesting information, and to save her from the risk of becoming blasée. When looking at the entrance from outside, the lion on the left, with its left paw on a cub, is the female symbolising the cycle of life and representing the yin; the lion on the right, with its right paw on a ball often carved with a geometric pattern, is the male signifying completion of things to perfection, and representing the yang. Their functions are to prevent evil spirits, or people with evil thoughts, from entering the premises, and to offer protection.

B cannot resist, she has to take pictures of the engraved wall plaque and of the lions. She has promised herself to keep a record of everything that happens during this trip, and to document it with the precise name of every location. Meanwhile, Alan and the group have gone through the tunnel-like entrance. They are inside the fortress compound and she must dash through the dark opening to catch up with them. But on the other side, she finds herself alone. All she can see in the alley bordered with walls are small plastic pandas perched on top of what could be rubbish bins, and more red lanterns hanging from metal arches. Where is everybody? The only way to find them is to shout, 'Where are you?' What a relief to hear Alan's voice close by, and be able to choose safely which way to turn to reach the parallel alley where they are waiting for her.

Nightmare over. Or maybe not. If it is a blessing not to be on her own any more, that does not mean that there are no more hurdles. Alan leads them up a short forty-five degree flight of stairs inside another dark tunnel cut through the thick wall that encircles the central area of the fortress. The best solution to carry the luggage up is for the whole group to form a human chain holding on to the providential handrail. Where does this testing passage lead? To a vast rectangular courtyard surrounded by low buildings with bay windows and sliding doors, both decorated with intricate wooden latticework painted in red, and with red lanterns dangling from the overhanging edges of the roof. It seems a miracle to find real human beings, not made of stone or plastic, in front of one of the doors. Standing to attention, three young girls in a red army-like uniform are watching the group in silence. They are the waitresses who will serve them their first Chinese cooked-in-China meal.

In the middle of that imposing courtyard, a large circular pool bordered by a low stone wall supporting at regular intervals small pots of red geraniums, provides a pleasing counterpoint to the angular symmetry of the whole building. Towering above it, a large weeping willow spreads its branches. It is bare of leaves but adorned with red lanterns hanging like ripe fruit.

B is tempted to take some pictures, but she has learnt her lesson and follows Alan closely. He is leading the group to their accommodation and much-needed relief from carrying heavy luggage. Actually, B is the only one who has very wisely planned to travel light, taking only bare essentials in her suitcase. The last-minute agony of removing articles just before leaving for the airport pays dividends now. She feels sorry for inexperienced members of the group who appear to be carrying ovens along with several changes of shoes and clothes.

They arrive finally in a large square courtyard, whose sides are four single-storey buildings divided into sections, each with a door and a window. It strikes her as typically Chinese, but at the same time a slightly disappointing feeling of déjà vu rises in her. It reminds her of the first Californian motel she saw decades ago when she travelled there with the English husband she had just married in Paris. Wherever you go on the globe, you carry with you the emotional baggage collected through the years. Some of it amuses you, some of it makes you wiser, some of it saddens you wherever you are.

But let us listen to Alan. He is haranguing the troops assembled around him, wishing them to enjoy everything they experience during this trip to China. They might have noticed the two lions at the entrance. They are there to protect you from evil. It is not entirely for aesthetic reasons that there is such a generous display of red everywhere. In China, since time immemorial, the colour red has been used to mean good luck, happiness, and joy. Here it conveys a welcoming message to guests, as is does all over China.

After these official words of greeting, he shows the members of the group the doors to their sleeping quarters. B has been assigned a twin bedroom to share with another single lady, fortunately as reserved and keen to keep her distance as is B. The room is small and with twin beds, or rather two wooden platforms with a thin mattress and some bed linen on each. To her amazement it has an en suite bathroom. After choosing their beds, the two of them agree tacitly on their reciprocal need to ignore each other. For each of them, having to spend nights in the proximity of another adult not related by marriage is a cross to bear. To their dismay, they find out next that their bathroom door has no lock, and does not even close properly. Let us leave them to sort out this thorny problem!

As if on cue, Alan calls everybody outside to take them to lunch. They are the only residents in the vast fortress-guest house. The dining room is empty and they occupy no more than two of the large circular tables. The centrepiece of each table is a big revolving lazy Susan that leaves only a narrow space in front of each guest, but allows them to pick and choose which food to put on their small plates. No fewer than ten different dishes are served on it. Compared with the food in most Chinese restaurants in England everything here is absolutely delicious. Instead of being too salty, swimming in burnt oil and reheated all day, it is freshly cooked and delicately flavoured with unusual seasoning. There is a variety of meats and chicken accompanied by vegetables, some of them local and unknown in Europe. After a while they bring as *pièce de résistance* a large river fish encased in a crisp brown crust that keeps its tail turned upwards. It is called a squirrel fish and would be worth a Michelin star anywhere. Tellingly, at the end of the meal not a crumb of food remains. Everyone leaves the dining room content and ready for their first walk on the Great Wall.

Outside, on the parking space, the coach is ready for them. It crosses the bridge straddling the dry river bed and climbs up the eastern side of the valley onto an empty tarmacked platform halfway up the slope. From the edge of it, one can see down below the village of Huangya Guan. At the other end an arched gateway with a couple of brick steps marks the entrance to the Great Wall. Everyone gets out of the coach. The driver unloads their walking equipment. It is not the time yet for Alan to explain today's programme and to display his knowledge of the region, as he had hoped to do on the coach during the morning. He leaps onto the top step to stand under the arch and addresses them in a commanding voice.

'Hey, here you need your walking boots. Walking poles are not essential, but if you are keen to use them they might help. And I recommend sunhats.'

'Alan, do you mind if I take your picture just where you are?' asks B, who is already pointing her camera in his direction. No need to equip herself for the walk. It is already done. She has been wearing her complete outfit of a well-seasoned mountaineer ever since she left home forty-eight hours ago, just in case her luggage did not arrive with the flight. Better safe than sorry.

In a few seconds, for the first time in her life, she is going to walk on the Great Wall of China. An uncontrollable excitement builds up inside her when she goes through the gateway to take her first steps on it. There it is, under her feet. Instinctively, she raises a finger to touch its parapet. As she does so an overpowering and enthralling feeling of communing with that massive construction seizes her and she submits to it, her eyes brimming with tears that she wills herself not to shed. It would be no exaggeration to say that what she is experiencing is as exhilarating for her as the moment painted by Michelangelo on the Sistine Chapel's ceiling, when God's finger brings Adam into being. Nothing has prepared her to be so transported. There are no precedents in her life. All she knows is that this heart-stopping moment will stay with her for ever.

Slowly, she returns to the real world and begins to take in the grandeur of the view before her. Arms stretched out along the parapet, she lets her eyes wander from the rising and falling waves of mountains in the hazy distance to the close jumble of ragged peaks sharply outlined against the bright sky. She gazes at the vast expanse of terraced foothills reaching far away beneath her. The Great Wall winds its way across that wild and chaotic scenery drawing bluish-grey streaks against the background. Its stone ramparts slither defiantly up and down the precipitous spine of a craggy hill, disappearing in a deep ravine to reappear higher up clinging to the top edge of a contorted outcrop of rocks. One section towards the left meanders off along a rising and dipping ridge before reattaching itself to the main body, while in the opposite direction another section levels out into a straight line that finishes abruptly when it crashes into an imposing cliff face of bare rock. In this landscape, mountain peaks join forces with the Great Wall to create an uninterrupted barrier and to establish a continuous line of defence.

There are no bird cries, no breeze rustling the leaves of the few trees strewn along the hillside. It is utterly still. At the bottom of the steep flight of steps in front of B, she can see a stretch where the Great Wall, levelling off along a ridge, supports an integrated watchtower perched on the edge of a sheer drop. Alan is already there with the group and waves to her. Throwing caution to the wind, she rushes down skipping every other step as she used to over rocks when she was mountaineering in the Alps. But that was half a century ago. At her age, how can she hope to arrive in one piece when she behaves so foolishly? Well, miraculously she does and catches up with them in a buoyant mood if slightly out of breath.

Alan does not look impressed, but refrains from criticizing her. He is too eager to seize his first real chance to enlighten the group. And she is grateful to have just enough time to get out her notebook and a pen before he begins to give some important information. This is roughly what she manages to scribble.

'This is a section of the Great Wall that was built in the sixteenth century during the last period of the Ming dynasty. The General Qi Jiguang designed this new type of Wall, made of stone and bricks, and extended it to the Yellow Sea. He also added watchtowers and garrison towers at regular intervals.

'Wall-building began in the second century BC with the First Emperor Qin Shi Huang Di who unified China. Over two thousand years China has had to deal with the problem of the northern nomadic tribes seen as barbarians. A Wall was the solution chosen by some Emperors to prevent the nomads from raiding the country. But the Wall had gaps and weak parts, and was never the impassable barrier it was meant to be. It is the longest man-made structure ever built and its Chinese name, Chang Cheng, means literally Long Wall. But it was never really a Great Wall. It failed to fulfil its mission of protecting the Chinese people.'

At this point in Alan's explanations, B stops writing, lost in her thoughts. Her pen pauses on the last word on the page. She is turning over in her mind what she has just heard about the Great Wall surviving to this day, and yet never able to protect the Chinese people as it was intended to do. In a moment brief as a flash of lightning she recognises that same failure in her own life. She too has survived to this day and has not achieved her purpose as a mother of leaving both of her children alive after her. The powerful feeling of communion with the Great Wall, that overwhelmed her when she first touched it, foreshadowed a link between its history and her personal story. Looking back at the fortuitous circumstances that brought her to China, she recognises in them a thread pulling her inexorably towards that revelation.

A mysterious bond unites her with that Great Wall unable to achieve its *raison d'être*. It has touched in her a sympathetic chord. They can both claim the right to view themselves as failures. With that formidable companion, she can share and reassess her deep sense of worthlessness. She stands transfixed, as if turning into redeeming stone in the stare of a Medusa. Already she feels that she is no longer adrift, no longer flotsam. Can her life return some day to its moorings?

In her heart, the words, *'la Grande Muraille de Chine'* sing a survivor's song. She murmurs to herself their trailing sonorities and hears them echoing along this massive construction. They seem to float away as they release the aural ballast of their French cadences. Was part of her already responding to the uncanny music of its French name when she decided one morning to leave behind the daily round to join this charity walk?

Such is the power of language. It explains her present need to silence everyday words and hollow remarks. The only conversation she wants to join is with herself. Why should she not let her thoughts play freely in her mind? As a bereaved mother, she belongs ineluctably to a world separate from the world of those spared such tragedies. And during these walking days, more than ever, she has to feel free to navigate in her parallel orbit, alone in her private capsule. She is simply unable to change course to join the group.

Still under the spell of the moment when the Great Wall revealed its secret meaning to her, B begins the walk towards the rest of her life. An exhilarating feeling of everything being as it should be propels her. Here the Great Wall asserts its presence, imposes a direction, prevents any false start. Its ramparts, in places as high as ten metres, the stone slabs of its walkway, feel even and safe under foot, and bring a spring to her step. Bounded securely by its brick parapets, she finds it liberating not to have to pick her way through unmarked countryside with the risk of getting lost. It is as easy as walking along a corridor, with the bonus of brilliant sunshine.

But after a few metres on the flat, the Wall takes off towards a rocky outcrop soaring high above the group of walkers and turns into an almost vertical stairway. On such a steep gradient, the Ming labourers chose to build steps with a normal tread depth but a much increased height for the risers, instead of adopting the opposite solution. It was imperative for the soldiers guarding the Wall to be sure of their footing if they had to move quickly to defend themselves against nomad assailants.

For the modern visitor, having to lift one foot after the other much higher than usual to reach the next step, amounts to an intensive total body workout. An added difficulty is that the steps are not uniform. Some are twice as high as others, and it is impossible to let your legs establish a rhythm. On the other hand, having to pay constant attention to where you place your feet is the best therapy to numb your mind to the pain of hamstrings burning on the way up and knees buckling on the way down. For B, concentrating her thoughts on the balls of her feet temporarily frees her mind of sad memories.

The NewShores group are the only people on the Wall today. Could the reason be that this first walk is nothing less than a daunting roller coaster of ascending and descending steps? There could not be a better test to filter out those who are badly trained and ill equipped. Even if her weeks of brisk walking on the treadmill at her local sports centre prove invaluable at this minute, she ought not to feel so superior. How about expressing some empathy? Can she not at least fake it? Obviously not, she has no time for such subtleties. A starting handle is cranking her up. This is what mountains do to her, whether they are in Europe or at the other end of the earth. She cannot wait for her walking boots to take her feet all the way to the top. Soon she falls in beside Alan and is striding at his pace.

The climb takes its toll on the group, spreading them out along this stony corridor. But they try to overcome the feeling of exhaustion and to keep going. After a while, just a few metres shy of the crest, their courageous efforts are rewarded. They find themselves in front of a large brownish dry stone construction that makes it impossible to go any further. It looks like a huge windowless and rusty beehive wedged tightly between the grey brick parapets, and blocking the way.

What a splendid opportunity to flop down on the steps of this dead end for a well deserved rest. It proves irresistible. Only Alan remains standing in front of that strange structure, like a teacher at a blackboard. His gaze sweeps over his captive audience and he smiles with satisfaction. They will just have to listen to his explanations. B, always hungry for more details, is already holding a pen on her open notebook when he begins.

'Here we have the only remnant of the original Huangya Guan Wall built in the sixth century during the Northern Qi Dynasty. At that time, there were only dry stone walls for which labourers had to extract rock from local quarries. They had the back-breaking task of carrying them from the valley floor to the top of these YanShan mountain ridges with an average altitude of over 700 metres. As I told you, ten centuries later, during the Ming Dynasty, this Huangya Guan Wall was reinforced with bricks and mortar and dressed stone, and watchtowers were added. It was an extraordinary feat of engineering.

'We're here on a two-kilometre Ming section that was repaired and renovated in 1985. The parapet on the enemy side is crenellated allowing a clear view of advancing attackers. Soldiers could survey the countryside, then shoot at invaders through the arrow slits and the spyholes below. In the parapet on the opposite side, there are openings with stairways at regular intervals to provide access to the rampart walkway.'

The sun is slowly disappearing behind the mountains, and the Great Wall is looking a shade darker when Alan stops talking and signals that it is time to move on. He begins to retrace his steps, making sure that everyone follows him. Soon they come to a junction in the Wall and take the fork that runs downhill to Huangya Guan, completing a strategic line of fortification with the outside walls of the fortress.

Here, the ground falls away very steeply towards the valley and the rampart is reduced to a narrow path high on the mountain ridge with a sheer ten-metre drop on one side plunging down into thick vegetation. Unlike the safe Ming walled-in corridor it is flanked on the right by a dry stone wall made of large ochre stones and recently-applied white plaster. In fact, that section looks like a modern version of a badly repaired Qi Wall with the recent addition of an iron handrail running along it. At the end of a very long day followed by a two-hour hike, it is difficult to find the surge of energy required to tackle safely that hazardous descent.

The group begins to file cautiously down the steep and perilous decline. Often, each of them has to grab the handrail quickly with both hands when their boots slide on loose gravel, and their walking poles become a nuisance. As there were no walking aids in her youth, B had learnt to trust her sense of balance to ramble safely and efficiently. She is glad that she has always refused to use walking poles. After much stumbling and staggering, with all kinds of contortions required to wedge one foot after the other between the wobbly stones strewn on the uneven ground, it is a minor miracle that no one requires hospital treatment. When they arrive on the road at the bottom of the slope, they can only manage to shuffle with every muscle aching along the two hundred metres to the Huangya Guan fortress.

At dinner that evening, no one has the energy left to turn the large lazy Susan loaded with food. Most of the small dishes are taken back to the kitchen untouched. Alan leaves a large thermos with boiling water at the door of each double room. Everyone retires to the privacy of their Chinese apartments. B and her companion discover that the only way to fill the empty cistern to flush their loo is to turn a little screw at the base of the pan. This has the immediate effect of flooding the whole floor of the bathroom before obtaining enough water for one flush. Thankfully their precious loo rolls, brought with them from England, are safely out of reach on the window sill.

But no more bathroom stories. Let us close the door on our exhausted walkers, both slumped on their beds inside their protective silk liners and sound asleep.

5½   Reflections

Oh, GM, I've got to talk to you. Nothing prepared me for such a day. I came to honour a deal I made with friends, 'If you help me to raise funds for NewShores, I promise to walk one hundred kilometres on the Great Wall.' That was my only purpose from the day I woke up saying to my husband, 'I am going to China.' It could be viewed as a leap in the dark. Oh, I know, for you there are no leaps in the dark. You know better, but you like to remain mysterious. It's not by chance that I call you the Great Mystery. You deserve it. Is GM too familiar? Well, after thirteen years together we don't need to stand on ceremony. I can talk to you as a friend.

What happened to me when I took my first step on the Great Wall today is almost impossible to describe. Euphoria is not too strong a word to express what came over me at the sight of it. I was mesmerised when I touched it for the first time. I could almost hear it telling me a story, a story that suffused me with joy because it was my story. Am I crazy, GM? Well, let me be for this trek. That magnificent Great Wall deserves it.

Did you make me decide to join that charity challenge? Were you scheming with Eric to shake me out of my years of torpor? Your strategy seems to be succeeding admirably, GM. I suppose it is working like an electric shock to a patient. Thank you, GM. You're giving me the unique chance to take an extraordinary journey that will leave me with beautiful and unforgettable memories. And now, 'La Grande Muraille' is going to play a part in my story. You and Eric will encourage me, and be with me all the way.

Already, I have so much to tell. China is casting a spell on me. Some might say that what I am enjoying is being taken out of my comfort zone. That's part of it, no doubt, but it's much more than that. Everything here fascinates me, enchants me. I love listening to Alan and learning about the Great Wall's role in the history of this huge country. My attempts to keep a detailed record of all I see and learn here are, of course, so that I can share it with my husband. I've never travelled without him, and never wanted to. Every minute I live through here is too enthralling, too rewarding to be wasted on me alone. But you know, GM, that that's only half the explanation.

Yes, knowing me inside out, you've guessed what I am going to say next. I feel that I do not deserve to enjoy even one minute of that trip. Why should I? How could I? This walking challenge was to raise funds and not, absolutely not, to have a good time. I'm here to fulfil my part of that contract, nothing else. But where is the challenge for me here? This Great Wall must relinquish its hold on my imagination, on my soul. I must remain as businesslike here in China as I was at home getting ready to go.

I am at a loss, GM. What's wrong with me? You'll have to help me sort out things in my heart and in my head. How can I accept that, for the first time in all these years, I am actually looking forward to tomorrow, but for reasons that I find contemptible?

6

The Huangyaguan Great Wall - West

B's first night in China is dreamless, uninterrupted, peaceful. As she wakes up, a feeling of panic invades her and she checks anxiously her travel clock. She dreads having to perform her morning ritual of getting ready in her present far-from-ideal circumstances. No time for a little snooze, it is already 6.30 am. She wriggles out of her silk liner, jumps down onto the floor, rushes to the bathroom and blocks its door with the suitcase that she has grabbed on the way. Now she can take out her pack of baby wipes and proceed to use them from head to toe, keeping the bottled water for brushing her teeth, as advised by Alan. She would not dream of touching the taps of the washbasin, or standing in the spacious wet room under the tiny shower head and pulling the cord, only to receive a deluge of slimy water. Clean and dressed for the day, she picks up the suitcase and opens the door. She finds her room-mate half-awake, rummaging in her many bags, and greets her with a cheerful, 'Good morning, it's all yours, I'm done,' before stepping discreetly outside.

The sun is shining and the mountain peaks surrounding her stand out sharply against the cloudless sky. Alan is already there placing a thermos of boiling water at each door. 'Good morning, B. Did you sleep well? The weather will be perfect all day for our walk.' B points a finger to the sky and replies, 'The weather's going to be perfect every day of this trip, Alan. My son is watching up there, keeping me safe and making sure that nothing can spoil my time in China.' After a brief pause, she hears the question that so few people ask, that always fills her with gratitude, 'What's his name?' She has to steady her voice before answering, 'Eric. It's really kind of you to ask, Alan. Thank you.' She inhales the fresh morning air deeply. She could cry out with joy to the blue April sky.

It is time to eat a copious breakfast to build up energy for the walk. The breakfast buffet is ready in the dining room, attractively displayed on a side table. To European eyes, the various slices of fluorescently-coloured vegetables on offer, together with the greyish steamed dumplings and stodgy buns of various sizes, look as though they need a government health warning. What a relief to find some thick pancakes with scrambled eggs on one of the serving dishes. As she piles some on her plate, she notices the three waitresses watching blankly. Is it not disgraceful of her to reject so openly food that is certainly unaffordable to their families? She goes back to the line and adds to her plate one small dumpling and one slice of one of the mysterious vegetables. What a mistake! One bite of that crunchy slice of pickled vegetable sets her tongue on fire, and causes her to regret her second thoughts. The burning will last all day, but the pancakes are delicious.

Outside, the tour leader, Emma, is gathering the trekkers for a quick warm-up session before the day's walk. By the end of the routine, a small group of elderly Chinese men has assembled, enjoying the spectacle of these aliens squatting and jumping on the spot, rotating their upper bodies, performing leg, arm and back stretches. When Emma insists on finishing with vigorous pelvic twisting and thrusting, it provokes hilarity among both the spectators and the actors.

All these warmed-up muscles and loosened joints are now

ready for action and it is Alan's turn to take charge of the group. He explains that they will set out on foot today and begin the western section of the Huangyaguan Great Wall. After a couple of hours, they will reach a very steep and famous stretch of two hundred steps called Heaven's Ladder. Sturdy walking boots are essential and poles might be useful.

While B is waiting for the group to get their act together, two elderly villagers approach her. One of them prods her in the chest, while raising his other hand with his little finger and thumb extended, then switching to a second puzzling gesture, making an 'L' with his thumb and index finger. As far as she is able to interpret their facial expressions and their inquisitive tone as they keep repeating the words, 'lee-o' and 'ba-a', they seem to be anxious to extract an answer from her. But what is the question? She can only shrug her shoulders and raise her eyebrows, hoping that her body language will demonstrate her incomprehension and encourage them to give up. But they do not, even when she adds a few noises in an attempt to sound eager but unable to play a more helpful role in this curious exchange. As a last resource, she indicates that they should stay while she consults her bilingual guide.

'Alan, come and help me, please. I haven't the faintest idea what these two old men want from me.' After a brief exchange with them, he turns to B laughing.

'They'd like to know if you are real?'

'Real?'

'Yes. They are saying 'lee-o' with the Chinese finger gesture expressing the number 'six', and 'ba-a' with the gesture representing the number 'eight', to mean sixty-eight. They have never seen a woman of that age who wanted to climb Heaven's Ladder, and they don't believe that such a woman could exist. They are asking you whether you are really that old.'

B had explained jokingly to the group in the coach the previous day that being sixty-eight she is the oldest among them, and that according to local customs she deserved to be venerated. In less than twenty-four hours, the message has been passed around as if in a game of Chinese whispers. For the first time in her life she feels the thrill of being a celebrity. Even if it is only in a small distant village, and for a limited time, fame is fame, and it is fun to taste it.

Why not make an amusing story out of it? She rummages in her daypack to extract her precious notebook and jots down a quick description of her little adventure. Suddenly the memory of a similar scene emerges. It is from a BBC programme on Dame Freya Stark at ninety that she saw several years ago. It showed that intrepid and indefatigable traveller in Tibet visiting a venerable Lama in the Himalayas and asking the guide why this holy man kept holding her hand and caressing it. 'He has never touched the skin of such an old woman before.'

B's unusual and hilarious experience of being deemed unique in the annals of Huangya Guan is worth storing in her treasure chest right away. Even if it will not make a television programme, she will have fun dining out on it in England.

At last everyone is ready to move on. They begin to walk towards the west on the road that runs along the outer wall of the fortress. At the foothills of the mountain, it becomes a Ming Wall flanked by the characteristic parapets built with bricks of varying shades of grey, and crenellated only on one side. In contrast, the patio-like surface of its walkway, made of large dusty slabs, looks rather drab and deceptively uniform. From time to time, a few low steps, often hard to detect in advance, interrupt the monotony, as if to remind the unwary to look at their feet instead of admiring the spectacular mountain scenery around them.

The ascent on this restored section of the Wall seems not much more than a gentle walk. Nothing as steep and arduous as yesterday. But not for long. Insidiously, the slope becomes steeper and slows them down, spreading them out according to their reserves of energy and the stiffness of their aching muscles. The real test comes when the gradient increases and the walled-in corridor becomes a demanding flight of high steps.

Why does B not seem to be affected by the climb? She is on drugs today. When she got up this morning, she knew that yesterday's walk, immediately after sitting for many hours in a plane and a coach, had taken its toll on her ageing muscles. So, she swallowed two tablets of an anti-inflammatory at breakfast. Not that she wanted relief from aching muscles. That is after all an essential part of the challenge for her. No, as a seasoned rambler she had recognised the signs of inflamed tendons and was terrified by the possibility of full-blown tendinitis invaliding her out of the trek. She is prone to that debilitating condition. Once it had completely ruined a walking holiday with her husband.

Halfway up the foothills heading towards high mountain ridges and crags, the group discovers that the restored Huangyaguan Wall terminates in a watchtower. It is a much appreciated opportunity for the group to pause for breath, rehydration, and camera action, and for Alan to provide them with useful information.

'We are leaving here the three-kilometre section of the Huangyaguan Great Wall that central government repaired in

1986,' he explains. 'You can see from here the first half that you did yesterday on the other side of the valley. You've just done the other half. Further on, you will see how the original Wall looks after centuries of natural decay. Many parts of it were damaged in the 1930s by the Japanese army, and more recently by the local peasants eager to use its stones to build their houses. Indeed, at one time, Chairman Mao encouraged them to do so.'

At this point, Alan stops talking. How could he add anything? The official line in China today is to insist that, thanks to Mao, nobody in China goes hungry. The Great Leap Forward, and the Cultural Revolution with its frenzy to destroy everything ancient, are not to be mentioned.

For the next few hundred metres the group cuts across an almost flat area of low scrub struggling to survive on dried-up greyish soil. When the Wall reappears, it is no longer clinging to the crest of a sheer mountain ridge. It is on a fifteen-metre high embankment topped with a crenellated parapet and reinforced on both sides by a fifteen-metre high retaining wall of rough-hewn stones of unequal sizes. The warm glow of their rich palette of orange and yellow lights up the scenery. Here and there, faded self-seeding plants cascade from the cracks. Leafless trees growing on the slope below are a sign that in a few months the view will be less arid.

Now they have to walk on the path at the base of that dry stone wall with loose soil and gravel crunching under foot. What a surprise to discover four packhorses tethered to the wall, waiting for customers and looking resigned to their lonely fate. Their owner is nowhere to be seen, and again today the

NewShores team and their Chinese guide are the only walkers on the Huangyaguan Great Wall.

The group welcomes the change from the restored Ming Wall with its even stone slabs between parapets of regularly aligned grey bricks. Eventually, they seem too constraining and predictable. This much older part of the Wall, that according to Alan dates back almost a thousand years, is strikingly different. It looks as if nature has been given free rein to demonstrate that man-made structures that are fit for purpose need not be austere. Nature has also demonstrated how such defensive structures are powerless against its repeated assaults.

Further on, an inaccessible jumble of crumbling ancient Wall, outcrops of natural rocks, and restored Ming Wall, roughly patched together, cling to the slope before disappearing into a thicket of scrub and vigorous conifers. They keep to the path, often difficult to trace, until it leads them through woods to the foot of a very steep hill. Alan walks ahead to stand by a tall menhir-like stone at the side of the track. He points to a column of Chinese characters carved on it and translates them as, 'Heaven's Ladder.'

At home, B had read those words in the description of the itinerary in the Trekkers World brochure. The biblical connotation had inevitably stirred up painful memories of wrestling with God. It had evoked in her disturbing images of standing at the foot of her own Jacob's ladder, with only the Angel of Death coming down to her. It had also reminded her of God's words to Jacob in Genesis 28, 'Behold, I am with you and will keep you wherever you go, and will bring you back to this land. For I will not leave you until I have done what I have promised you.' A promise that had proved cruelly empty.

There was also a lyrical quality in the name 'Heaven's Ladder' that had enchanted her. It had conjured up visions of the heavenly scenes depicted by so many great Renaissance painters. Today, standing at the foot of that sixty-metre high stone ladder, it looks more hellish than heavenly. That only needles B, making her welcome the challenge. She is now eager to experience the exhilaration of tackling such a demanding task. No surprise that those two Chinese villagers were amazed that a woman of her age would attempt to reach the top.

Alan's earlier warnings have not prepared the trekkers for the daunting climb ahead. They survey apprehensively the nearly vertical wooded hillside cut by a narrow gully filled with rough stones. It chisels a gap in the dark outline of the hilltop against the bright sky. Allan adds teasingly, 'A mere sixty metres, two hundred steps, no more, and then you'll be on a nice platform at the top admiring the panorama.'

The awesome sight of these two hundred steps cleaving the wooded hillside brings out B's fighting spirit. This steep flight of poorly assembled crumbling stones galvanizes her. She did not expect to feel so strong, so eager to confront and to shoulder aside her old demons. Something, someone, yes someone, makes her feel invincible.

With Alan leading the way, the group rushes to begin the ascent, so as to get it over quickly. After the first few rungs of roughly-hewn blocks of stone propped unevenly against the steep hillside, what begins as a tight Tour de France *peloton* unravels. Some have to lean hard on their walking poles, but simply get them stuck in the cracks between the stones. Some have to pull themselves up by holding on to the rusty handrails on either side. Some choose to chat, exchange jokes, giggle, and soon stop, breathless. The distance between the climbers increases steadily.

But how is B getting along? She is almost half-way up Heaven's Ladder, counting under her breath, '...95, 96, 97...' The precise figure of two hundred steps announced by Alan sounded like the words of a contract. She never signs a contract before examining its terms. Has he been exaggerating, throwing in that round number to terrify the group? Can she prove him wrong? Giving herself pointless tasks, as she is doing now, is her way of creating a personal wall against unwelcome thoughts. Over the years, she has become expert at it. Alan's words have taken her by surprise and awoken memories of a tiny hand holding hers on the vertiginous stairs of the Eiffel Tower, and her voice saying, 'Let's count, shall we?'. She must block them out before they bring tears.

Her counting game offers other advantages. It helps her to stop grumbling, 'Why, Oh why, are my legs so short?' each time she has to tug at her trouser leg to lift her foot to the next high step. Following the rhythm of the counting allows her leg muscles to work in harmony with her breathing, ideal for keeping a steady pace. As one would expect, it helps to strengthen her determination not to slow down, even when the height of the steps and the gradient have increased drastically. Perhaps it is also a matter of pride for her, the same pride that she felt in her mountaineering days fifty years ago, when those same legs could climb rocky peaks in the Alps, or jump across icy crevasses. The illusion that she could walk effortlessly for ever is exhilarating. She has passed the test. She is her intrepid and tireless young self again.

'...182, 183, 184...' The finish line is near. Still no need to hold on to the handrails of this seemingly endless flight. She keeps her eyes firmly fixed on the uneven and often broken steps. She finds her second wind. Her pace accelerates. It is as if winged heels are lifting her Mercury-like to the top.

Now she is flying. Is there a voice calling her from the top, encouraging her? '...199,' and now '... 200'. She steps onto the small platform at last. It feels as if she has reached Heaven, and the promise of an impossible encounter is being renewed. This intense experience has no precedent in her life.

Her blind gaze lost in the shadows of the past, she stands, communing with herself for a few precious moments. The spell breaks. Her eyes sweep slowly across the awesome mountainous peaks around her. It is time to act again as if she belongs to the group. She greets each one as they arrive on the small platform, feeling proud of what they have achieved. When they are all there she takes part wholeheartedly in the loud mutual congratulations. She is smiling with them when Alan takes pictures to immortalise their exploit

Afterwards, leaning safely against the parapet, she looks down at the plunging view where in the distance Huangya Guan's houses and converted fortress are children's toys. High above the village, range upon range of ever fainter bluish mountains ripple to the horizon edged against the blazing sky. What a privilege to immerse herself in the immensity and grandeur of such a breathtaking panorama. She is overwhelmed, transfixed. A voice from her Germanist past at the Sorbonne resonates in her. Like Faust, she feels impelled to say, *'Verweile doch! Du bist so schön!'* 'Stay a while, you are so beautiful!'

However much she dreads the jollity of the group, it is as selfish as foolish to desire to be left alone with the mountains right now. Instead, she screws up her eyes in an attempt to fix their image in her mind. In vain. What radiates around her cannot be captured as a permanent memory. The only solution is to trust her camera. She takes a few pictures, thrilled at the prospect of having these stunning views as posters when she returns to England. She will hang them on her kitchen wall and keep them as lasting reminders.

She imagines herself back at home re-living these extraordinary moments. Is she aware yet of how much they will have changed her? She cannot be. Every day we weave the fabric of our life not knowing what pattern it is following, or even who designs it for us.

It is time to set off again after a relaxing pause on the platform at the top of Heaven's Ladder. Prolonged effort at a steady pace always leaves B feeling invigorated and eager for more. She would like to run now, but it would be unwise to confess that to the group, while some are still aching from their ordeal. She really ought to act her age.

When they start walking again, they follow a more or less even path uphill, cutting across an area of gorse and dishevelled bushes. It is a relief not to have to watch constantly where they put their feet. Suddenly they hear an eerie plaintive voice singing a sad song. Everyone stops, mesmerised by that haunting Chinese tune and its invisible singer. The suspense is over when they find behind an overgrown bush a small woman crouching beside a gigantic box twice her size. She gets up hastily without a word and begins to walk with them blithely carrying the box strapped to her back. It does not seem to require any effort from this incredibly strong Chinese who slows down only when someone in the group gets in her way.

After a climb of a few hundred metres through colourless undergrowth, the view opens out. But where is the Great

Wall? All they see in front of them is an amalgam of washed-out brown earth and greyish stones, a rugged ridge rising a few metres above the hilltop. It stretches along the ground like the bloated corpse of a dragon spiked with sharp rocks. Soon the path runs along the top of that steeply ascending ridge with sheer drops on either side. This one-metre wide track is not for the fainthearted. One misstep and she would tumble downhill on either side into an entanglement of bare saplings, gorse and bushes. Would it cushion her fall and prevent immediate death, wonders B. Her old mountaineering instinct to assess risk before tackling a tricky passage never deserts her. She still recalls how essential it is to minimise the danger of tripping.

Progressively, the risk of a soft landing with just a few scratches turns into real danger, as the drop on either side increases and large boulders protrude from the vegetation. The mountain resembles a vast playground for a game of *pétanque* played by giants hurling huge rocks. After a few hundred metres, the column of walkers slows to a halt when the narrow track is blocked by a couple of large boulders. Alan ponders how best to solve the problem of getting past them with a group of mature people of rather varied fitness.

'You'll have to give us a leg up, Alan,' suggests the heaviest girl of the group laughing. Adroitly, he manages to avoid using the proposed solution. He places one foot in a small crack in the rock as a temporary foothold, and reaches the top in a single jump. From that safe position it is easy for him to take command. Securely wedged between the two boulders, he hauls up each of the trekkers.

When B's turn comes, she grasps asperities in the rock, convinced that she can scramble to the top by herself, as she has done so many times in her mountaineering past. Alas, the past was more than five decades ago! After a few pathetic attempts, she has no choice but to take Alan's hand and be pulled up unceremoniously like the rest of the group. Her I-can-do-it attitude has received such a battering that she is unable to thank Alan and laugh off the episode, as have all the others. She looks mortified; in fact she is sulking. If only there were a mirror, one look at it would persuade her not to behave like a spoilt child. The giggling group decides wisely to leave her alone. We had better do the same.

But, look. After a while her face lights up and she starts laughing silently. Is she recovering her dignity already? No, she is replaying in her mind this morning's hilarious scene with the old men on the forecourt of Huangya Guan fortress. She is in a good mood again. No more hard feelings. She is even able to witness without envy the little Chinese woman climbing unaided over the boulders that have just defeated her. B cannot believe her eyes when she sees her running along the path winding up to a dilapidated tower, where she places her box on the ground.

When she removes its top it turns out to be a rudimentary padded icebox, out of which she extracts four or five large bottles of Coca-Cola and at least twenty cans of fizzy drinks, before waiting quietly for customers. It beggars belief that such a heavy load could be carried uphill for hundreds of metres by such a small woman. She must have the genes of those labourers conscripted to carry stone slabs from the valley to the mountain crest to build the Huangyaguan Great Wall.

Everyone rewards her efforts by purchasing most of her portable bar. If she deserves to be paid for her *tour de force*, they feel entitled to a cold drink. All things considered, it is a fair deal. As soon as they start moving, she collects the empty bottles and cans, shoulders her box and follows them. To everyone's relief the path now runs across a flat area along the edge of a pine forest and then follows the contours of a bare hill.

Just when it becomes enjoyable to stride unhindered by gravity, Alan makes everyone stop for a picnic lunch. They sit on the grass eager to taste the cucumber and ham sandwiches, and the cakes provided by the guest house. Will that be an ordeal for their European taste buds? No, they are delicious. While they are eating, it feels awkward to be watched by the silent Chinese woman standing stoically beside her open box, now with a display of books, postcards, T-shirts and bracelets of coloured beads at her feet.

'Shouldn't we buy some of her stuff?' asks someone. Alan's reply, 'You don't have to,' seems mean to B. 'But surely, Alan, she has made a tremendous effort to get here. We should do something for her in return.' His apparent lack of empathy is hard to understand, until he explains it. 'People in this village haven't yet become greedy and eager to exploit tourists. It would be wrong to spoil them. You should have a look at what she is selling, and buy from her only if you wish to. And don't pay her more than she is asking.'

Rummaging among the T-shirts, and being unable to find anything smaller than 'extra-large', B does not have the heart not to buy one. It is only weeks later back in England that she will dare to try it on and look at herself in the mirror. The hugely oversized and shapeless T-shirt proclaiming in bold Chinese characters and in English, 'I climbed the Great Wall,' is quite a sight. Enough to make her granddaughters giggle when she models it for them.

After hours of steep ascent, it is a joy to see the path following the foothills of low mountains softly outlined against the sky. The trail dips slightly downhill beside the Wall now reduced to a thin line of rubble that snakes across an almost flat expanse of grass and gorse. It is as low as half a metre, rising hardly to a metre on its uphill side, and the stones at the top are loose and unstable. In places, blocks have spilt over the track. It looks like a demolition site. They have no choice but to walk on the grass beside it.

At first, the descent seems undemanding. But actually it puts strain on knees and ankles, and makes it difficult to keep one's balance when the slope becomes steeper and gravel replaces grass. How grateful she is to have thought of having her old walking boots resoled with Skywalk Vibram, the type of soft sole that grips better than more hardwearing ones. She can trust them on rocks, scree or treacherous gravel, and with their old-fashioned thick leather they feel as protective as armour around her ankles. She remembers how well these faithful companions have served her over the years. Together they have climbed countless mountains, she will never let them retire.

Predictably, two inexperienced members of the group slide down a patch of dry earth and fall heavily on the most padded part of their body. When another one stops at the top of the steep slope, petrified, unable to decide how best to use her walking poles for support, B rushes back to grab her arm saying, 'Why don't you give me your walking poles and hold on to me? I am quite stable with my walking boots and I have years of mountaineering behind me.' The immediate reply, 'I am all right. Move away, please. It makes me nervous to have you behind me like that,' takes her aback. She realises that her offer to help may have been seen as patronising and feels badly about it. She should not flaunt her experience of trekking and mountaineering.

It takes at least an hour to descend to the bottom of a narrow valley where three small single-storey houses huddle together among a few stunted trees. Two of them have broken windows and seem unoccupied. They are possibly used for storage. The third is built along three sides of a square courtyard. Each section has large timber-framed bay windows that look out on the inner courtyard while the outside walls are windowless. The top half of each door is a window, as in elegant French apartments. But this is a small mountain village, and despite the obvious efforts of the poor farmers who live here to turn it into a kind of guest house, it cannot be compared with France. There are three tiny double bedrooms with just enough space to put a cheap double bed base. Next to them, a large wooden base to accommodate up to five guests occupies a slightly larger dormitory. Bedding is provided in the form of paper-thin mattresses and old duvets. The lavatory is a small hut outside the courtyard, next to a pig sty.

This feels like the real challenge for which so many generous friends have sponsored B. This is what she was hoping for. She could not be happier. The fresh local produce cooked for dinner by the farmer's wife tastes heavenly. The left section of the couch shared with her room-mate could not be more comfortable. Never mind that the curtains are impossible to close. She feels at peace with the world when Morpheus takes her into his arms.

6½ Reflections

I feel badly, GM. I was meant to go to China to take on a charity challenge in memory of Eric, not to enjoy myself in these stunning mountains, today even more than yesterday. It shouldn't have been such a fantastic day. If only I'd realised that signing up for that challenge would be nothing more than an excuse to hide behind a façade of altruism while having a wonderful time. You should never have let me use Eric's life for my own benefit. You know each of us inside out. Couldn't you tell that it would make me despise myself for being a cheat? Well, that's exactly what's happening now.

Of course, a day like today is bound to take me back into the past, and to wake up all sorts of memories. It fans those burning questions that have no answers. Why do you spoil me with good knees that still function perfectly, when Eric had to suffer stoically from painfully stiff knees from the age of sixteen? It hurts me so much when I remember how it prevented him from playing any sports like his peers, and worse, when I think of how it ruined his dream of fencing in the Olympics. Why did it happen to him and not to me? He didn't deserve it. It's so unfair. I simply can't come to terms with it. Oh, how I wanted him to know the joy of following his dream. And don't tell me that I can't regret a fantasy. After winning tournament after tournament, he was judged good enough to enter the ranks of those competing at the top. It meant so much to him.

How do you think it feels seeing myself strutting and spreading my plumage on this stunning Great Wall, while Eric is condemned never to have such an experience? It's wrong the way things are, all wrong. Don't we both know that? As long as you won't give me an explanation, I'll never find it anything but wrong. That will never change for as long as I can draw breath.

In a sense, you managed to inflict some kind of punishment on me today, to make me serve time for it. I had to carry my constant tormentors, the familiar trinity of remorse, guilt and regret sitting on my shoulders, and they felt heavier than usual. My legs climbed easily the two hundred steps of that stone Ladder but it was no Jacob's Ladder for me. There were none of your angels ascending and descending to bring me hope. And how could there be? You didn't look after Eric when he went on his year out, you didn't bring him back alive to England. If there was an angel on the Ladder with me today, it was the Angel of Death. Thank God, I was not asleep in the desert. I prefer to meet my dreams wide awake, especially bad dreams that turn out to be true.

To be fair, GM, you did one positive thing for me on that Ladder. Yes, you did, perhaps out of pity. You made me count the steps, and the higher the number the stronger I heard a voice. It was the voice of Eric. I knew that he was climbing those steps ahead of me and calling me with words of encouragement, as he did when he was seven and we climbed together the stairs of the Eiffel Tower. There's no Heaven on earth, I know. But you took me close to one today. I am grateful to you for those precious moments, GM. I'm keeping them in my treasure chest.

And thank you also for this crazy encounter with my two Chinese admirers. If only I could read and understand Chinese! I can imagine the headline in the Huangya Guan Gazette tomorrow, 'Amazing elderly Western woman climbs Heaven's Ladder.' Hope you take it with a pinch of salt when I am bursting so unashamedly with silly pride. I need a dose of *humour to give some flavour to my life and its sorrows, and it never leaves me with a bad aftertaste. As you can tell, GM, I was in real need of something, anything, to make me feel a little less worthless.*

On balance, GM, I ought to thank you for today. I hope it allows you to sleep well tonight, as I am sure I shall do. I'll be back tomorrow.

7

The Great Wall at Qian Gan Xian

B had fallen into deep sleep so quickly last night that, when she wakes up in the dark, her first thought is that she is having another of those two-hour periods of insomnia that have plagued her for years. She has a torch, but no book to read herself to sleep with. When she consults her travel clock, it is a relief to see that it is 5.30am. Someone, somewhere, has adjusted her internal clock, so that she can be up early enough to avoid the embarrassment of a lack of privacy. All her adult life, changing rooms at swimming pools or sports centres, and communal fitting rooms in shops have made her feel painfully ill at ease. Today, under cover of darkness, wrapped in her anorak and holding her torch, she tiptoes across the courtyard, opens the low gate, and scuttles towards the small hut near the pigsty. Suddenly, violent banging makes her jump. It is the old sow letting her know that she is protecting her ten piglets. A couple of flustered chickens try to fly out of their enclosure. No one else around, she can relax.

Back in her bedroom, she crouches in the small space between the edge of the bed and the wall, and performs her morning ritual with the baby wipes as quickly and silently as possible before getting dressed. Fortunately her room-mate is still asleep when she finishes. It is daylight outside now, but no sign of anyone getting up. There are two large metal cylinders on the roof of the room across the courtyard, so she decides to go and see if they are a water supply connected to the internal plumbing. Impossible to peep inside that room because of the half-closed curtain. She opens the door carefully, holding her toothbrush and her bottled water, but retreats immediately. It is actually the one and only bathroom for the guests and the inhabitants of the farmhouse. One of them is standing at the tiny washbasin splashing water on his face. Better to flee outside to gaze at the stunning mountain scenery around her, with the sun rising in the intense blue of the sky.

She notices a group of peasants on a patch of bare ground at the bottom of the small slope just below the farmhouse. One of them is cutting furrows, pushing a small wooden plough harnessed to the bent back of another man who is pulling it slowly like a beast of burden. Following them, a woman holding a bucket is sowing seeds. Catching sight of B watching them, they gesture cheerfully inviting her to join them. It would have been fun, but she points at her watch to indicate that she cannot spare the time. However, she cannot let such a photo opportunity pass. She waves her camera at them to see if they turn away. No, they are quite happy for her to take a picture of them smiling proudly. She thanks them with a grateful 'xièxiè', hoping that she is not using a Chinese tone that changes her 'thank you' into an incongruous word.

By now, the courtyard is filling up with members of the group exchanging jokes about the sleeping arrangements. Jimmy, the young GP, shows everybody the earplugs he has brought with him. They are vital, as he has been assigned the double room with the only other single man in the group. They enjoy each other's company, except at night when the older one begins to snore as soon as he closes his eyes. The female dormitory must also have been quite noisy. This morning, the five women sharing it can hardly keep their eyes open. Bravely, one of them decides to have a shower when the bathroom is free. She emerges with her hair dripping; she describes how some water had trickled down on her from one of the containers on the roof, but that it was cold and brownish. Morning ablutions are better reduced to a strict minimum.

Later, in the dining room, while eating a breakfast consisting again of a delicious galette of fried eggs between thin pancakes, B asks Alan, 'What's the name of this village? I like to take pictures with the name of where we are, but I couldn't see any signs around here.' 'It's the mountain village of Qian Gan Xian. It's higher than Huangya Guan. You can feel that the air is colder and the sun stronger. Today we do a three-hour walk climbing from here, and then we come down to the road and the coach takes us to our next stop. Leave your luggage in the courtyard outside your bedrooms. And now, no time to lose, let's go!'

But first things first. Emma insists again on assembling everyone in the courtyard for a vigorous warm-up session before leaving. Hiking with cold muscles in the cold mountain air would be a mistake. Afterwards, they set out on a very steep path just above the farmhouse at the edge of cultivated terraces carved into the slope. Dotted here and there, small white-blossomed trees sparkle in the sunshine. The red-brown soil is dry but recently hoed, though hardly anything is growing at this time of year.

After a climb of about five hundred metres, they leave the terraces where they have had to tiptoe with dainty little steps to avoid damaging future crops. They begin to stride purposefully across fields to reach the Wall. They are high above the farmhouse and the view opens up into a wide arena of soft-contoured hills. The thin line of the Wall meanders along their undulations. It has shrunk to a ghost of its original self. In many places, it rises no higher than a metre and its parapets have been eroded away. Its reptilian spine with debris scattered along its edges is not much of a path, but B and a few others choose to hobble on this unstable and uneven surface with the risk of wedging their feet in the treacherous gaps between the blocks of stone. Others prefer the relative safety of coarse grass and tussocks growing alongside, and struggle when they have to step over bare patches strewn with loose stones.

It seems to go on and on, and finally becomes so tiresome that B decides to pause to let everyone pass her. Viewed from below, the sweeping curve of the narrow wall skirting the ridge of the hill, with the line of walkers silhouetted against the bright sky, reminds her of Ingmar Bergman's film, 'The Seventh Seal'. Here they are balancing precariously as if walking barefoot on burning coals. Ahead of them, Alan strides confidently to the top of the hill. She remembers the time when friends would call her a mountain goat. Such an expression no longer fits her but describes him perfectly.

He waves at her, pointing to something red looming over the edge of the hill. Could it be the roof of a Chinese café serving cold drinks? Everyone accelerates and discovers that they have reached the highest point of the hills. On the other side, the ground drops away steeply, offering an impressive view over a vast expanse of lower plains and valleys stretching into the distance. That explains the table and two long concrete benches sheltered by a large sheet of red corrugated metal supported by high poles. It really is the ideal spot to rest and to admire the panorama.

A low triangular stone marker next to that gazebo-like construction also seems an excellent place to sit and gaze at the impressive scenery. Alan stands next to it, looking at the group with an expectant expression that makes them fall momentarily silent. It is the signal for B to take out her pen and notebook. Now he can share with them his knowledge of the Wall's history. Let us listen to him.

'Today, it has only been a three-hour walk on the Huangyaguan Great Wall. In these first three days you've walked more than half of its 42 kilometres, and climbed as high as 750 metres. Well done.

'The first Wall-building period on a massive scale was in the second century BC with the First Emperor Qin Shi Huang. Then, in the sixth century, Wall building started again seriously with the Emperor of the Northern Qi dynasty who created a line of defences from the Yellow River to the Yellow Sea. And finally, in the sixteenth century, during the last period of the Ming dynasty, the General Qi Jiguang persuaded the Emperor to reinforce and extend the existing Walls with a new method of construction using stone and bricks.

'The Huangyaguan Great Wall is a unique site and a fantastic history lesson. As I told you yesterday, you have here stretches of the sixth century Northern Qi Wall, renovated and reinforced in the sixteenth century during the late Ming dynasty. A three-kilometre section was repaired again by central government between 1984 and 1986. And you have also seen in a few places, left unrestored, the original Northern Qi Wall, which uses the dry stone walling and rammed earth method. It was a way of taking advantage of local resources, rather than making millions of bricks, demanding a much larger workforce.

'This marker is called the Three Province Stone because we are here at the junction of Beijing municipality, Hebei province and Tianjin municipality. Beijing is one hundred and thirty kilometres to the west.

'OK. Now we're off on a good path down to a road that we follow for a few kilometres to find our coach. And the coach will take us to our next stop.'

During these explanations, B has been scribbling as fast as she can. If only she knew how to use the top-of-the-range digital mini-recorder she bought especially for the trip four days ago at Heathrow airport. Everyone has volunteered to help her to understand its instructions booklet, but it baffles them all. Young children would know instinctively which buttons to press, and would understand the mysterious numbers appearing on the tiny screen.

History was never her favourite subject, and she rarely reads biographies. Nevertheless, she should have made the effort to refresh her basic knowledge of China's history before the trip. All these Qi and Qin and Ming are so confusing for the ignorant trekker that she is! But she is resolved that it should not remain so. Where does this sudden interest come from? Why is she so eager to learn more about the Great Wall and its two thousand years of tribulations? What is happening to her? Since losing Eric, the present pins her malevolently to the sorrows of the past. Something is waking her from that evil spell. This trek gives her the strength to live every moment intensely. Learning about the past makes her a participant in an infinitely greater context. Growing in her, she discovers the will to free herself. At this spot, where the stone marker points towards three provinces, a new direction is opening up for her.

As promised by Alan, it is easy to follow the short path down the wooded hillside to the valley and the road. Walking on the flat and on tarmac feels strange now. But it allows everyone to concentrate on the view rather than their feet. Nothing lush or green in that bare and bone-dry countryside. There are no fields here to till. Small ramshackle single-storey farmhouses without the characteristic courtyard are the mark of a poverty-stricken rural area. But most of them have, near their entrance doors, a stack of new bricks allocated to each inhabitant by local government to demonstrate its generosity. No sign of mechanised farming. Bundles of dried corn husks lie scattered on the ground together with various farming hand tools. The farmers must be away working.

A few sheep and a lonely cockerel are the only signs of life. Small wooden ladders protrude from narrow holes dug deep into the ground to provide natural cold storage. Electricity is still scarce in poor rural China. At last the group walks past an old man standing beside a small open truck full of fruit and vegetables, with a primitive balance made of a bamboo pole resting on his shoulders with pans dangling from each end.

It is a sad truth universally acknowledged by every traveller that any part of the world showing hardship and deprivation is a photographer's paradise, and can be considered a rightful opportunity to produce beautiful pictures. Our NewShores group sees it as the business of their short time in China to indulge in the pleasures of that paradise.

When the road leads through a small village, B shows no restraint, quick to seize the moment to take unusual pictures for her scrapbook. A row of two-storey houses, with some of their windows criss-crossed with wooden planks or bricked up, look like slums. But old signs advertising Coca-Cola in English indicate that there are shops behind the broken-down façades. On the pavement in front of one of them stands an old billiard table with faded baize and a couple of cues in fair condition. It is hard to tell whether the few elderly people along the wall behind it are there to watch a possible game, or because there is nothing else to do. They do not turn away or hide their faces behind their hands when B takes a picture. It is only later, at home, that she will regret her lack of respect. Being keen and in a hurry to snap something unusual was no excuse for not asking their permission. Right now such considerations are far from her mind. Anything surprising and new is fair game.

Further on, in a slightly less depressed part of the village, a small van packed with smartly dressed young men stops next to her. She is more amused than intrigued when one of them gets out and strikes a pose full of bravado in front of her saying, 'Take picture of me.' To the delight of his friends, she obeys, and they drive away laughing and shouting bye-byes. Unfortunately, B's camera does not allow her to delete the picture immediately. She has to have it printed with all the others when she gets back home and can only then throw it away.

A few minutes later, she catches sight of their familiar coach amid the slow traffic of three-wheelers and old trucks. No need to walk any more to reach the next destination. Just a couple of steps to climb aboard and collapse into a comfortable seat. What luxury! She is looking forward to the drive and the opportunity to discover more countryside. How quickly fades the compassion she felt for the poor people she has left behind sitting in their old chairs expecting nothing from life.

This time, she is going to stay awake during the trip and watch carefully everything that goes by outside. If only she had known what a nerve-racking experience the two hours on that coach would be, she would have preferred to sleep. Either the driver is crazy, or he has no brakes. He never slows down. He thinks himself the Emperor of the road. No other vehicle is allowed to pass. Fortunately, there is little traffic on that country road, but it is often narrow, or has sharp curves. When he suddenly weaves around a motionless peasant sprawled in the road beside his toppled three-wheeler, and fails to stop or even slow down, everyone screams in protest, 'Stop, we can't leave him, he might be dying.' But what is one person's life worth to him in a country of a billion?

When they leave the country road to take the motorway through the outer suburbs of Beijing, the only improvement is the relative safety of separate lanes, with their speed limits freshly painted on the tarmac. Whenever the various three-wheeled vehicles and old trucks succeed in reaching the fast lane, they stay obstinately in it, confining the coach and all the more powerful cars to the slow lane. Overtaking other vehicles on the wrong side seems to be a standard manoeuvre in the coach driver's repertoire.

When mountains begin to rise on the horizon, B takes her gaze from the road and lets her eyes wander right and left to admire the view. Alan picks up the microphone.

'You've noticed all these orange and green banners floating on poles along the road. They are for the Peach Blossom Festival. It's on at the moment in the Pinggu District of Beijing. But now we're in the Gubeikou mountain range and we're going through its main pass. You can see the Crouching Tiger Mountain on the left, and the Coiling Dragon on the right. In Chinese, Wohu and Panlong. In about twenty minutes, you'll be in Jinshanling where we stay two nights.'

After a two-hour drive, it is exciting to arrive at a new destination. The coach stops in front of an open gate with walls on either side. Everyone inside gets ready to leave the coach. But what is happening outside? Pandemonium breaks out as a pack of about fifteen women fight their way towards the door of the coach while five young boys in khaki uniforms battle to push them away, to open up a passage for the group. They are all shouting at each other. The women are yelling and pointing fingers at the boys, as if they are telling them to stop being a nuisance. The boys stand their ground, yelling back at them, but appearing not entirely sure of what to do next. Then, as quickly as it started, everything stops, no more threatening gestures, no more screaming. Loud laughter erupts in both camps, followed by cheerful exchanges. Everything seems forgotten. It was all theatre. The performance is over, the actors are all smiles. Alan reassures the dumbfounded audience that it is perfectly safe to come out of the coach, and that he will explain it all to them later.

While everyone sorts out their bags and suitcases as the driver unloads them, a young woman comes towards B to grab her hand and say with an engaging smile, 'I am your friend. I like you. I help you.' B is amazed to be greeted in English. 'I am your friend, too. I like you also. Thank you.' She is deeply moved by this friendly welcome and wants the woman to feel that she should not feel guilty about what happened a few minutes ago. Then the woman pushes forward a tiny girl who was hiding behind her and tugging at her sleeve. 'My daughter, she is five, her name is Li Hua, my name is Ling.' B bends down to the girl's level and clasps her in her arms exclaiming, 'Hello, Sweetie.' Terrified, the little Li Hua wriggles out of her embrace and retreats behind her mother. 'Me, grand-mother,' explains

B, holding one hand with extended fingers and gesturing with the other to indicate the respective heights of her five granddaughters. Ling nods a few times with a puzzled expression on her face and all of a sudden smiles broadly, 'Ah, you, Naa Naa!'

Why would she call her Nana? **B** has never let anybody call her by that name; she dislikes it. She uses the title of *Grand-Maman*. But she must admire a young Chinese woman living in a remote village in the mountains who is able to speak some English and even knows words of little practical value like 'Nana'. So, she agrees joyously pointing at herself, 'Yes, I am a Naa Naa.' It is only when she tells that story to Alan that she learns that 'Naa Naa' is actually the Chinese word for grandmother. Why didn't she realise that? She will also realise later the reason for Ling's intriguing and apparently spontaneous declaration of friendship.

The little girl shows signs that she wants to leave, and her mother takes her away waving good-bye and smiling engagingly. It is time for **B** to pick up her suitcase and follow the group. But where is everyone? Once again she is guilty of lingering behind. She is incorrigible. Well, why not allow her to live every minute of that trip to the full? Everything since she arrived in China is so interesting and exciting.

She rushes through the gate and is relieved to find the group gathered around a spreading willow tree in one corner of a wide courtyard. At the back of it there is a large single-storey building with bay windows all along its façade. A few enticing tables with parasols and white metal chairs are scattered outside. When Alan appears at the side of the building he explains that it is the communal dining room, but there is no time to relax as he needs to show them their lodgings.

They follow him with their luggage through an intricate network of narrow alleys bordered by two-metre high brick walls. Doors let into these walls at regular intervals give access to small walled courtyards with two double bedrooms built along the side facing the door. When Alan indicates their respective bedrooms, he points out that the courtyard doors have no numbers to identify them. The group has to remember how many right and left turns they need to take to reach them. An impossible challenge for B. She has no sense of direction and can get lost, with or without a map, as soon as she ventures more than three streets away from home.

Her double bedroom and en suite bathroom look familiar. They are similar to the ones they had for the first night, but slightly less run-down. No need to spend time examining them. She hears chattering and laughter. She encourages her room-mate to come with her to join whoever is outside in the alley, and to follow them to the main courtyard. That way, they arrive safely in the huge dining room. They do not have to wait long before a delicious dinner is served. It is composed of the same meat and vegetable dishes that they have enjoyed the first two nights. Everything perfectly flavoured and artistically presented with a predominance of red food like tomatoes and chillies.

The plaque at the entrance of the Huangya Guan fortress said 'Huangya Mountainvilla Guesthouse'. Here the sign says 'Jinshan Hotel'. And indeed the place feels slightly more upmarket. So, why is it that once again they are the only guests? It is sad that tourists are unaware of the attractions of the Great Wall far from the huge crowds of the restored sections closer to Beijing. If only the NewShores team of volunteers could appreciate how lucky they are to be here in 2005; before the 2008 Olympic Games; before tourists begin to invade the breathtaking solitude and silence of these remote sections of their trek, and spoil them for ever.

After the meal, Alan explains what the earlier commotion was about. In China today, every eighteen-year-old male fit for compulsory military service must serve for two years. Their tasks are those of policemen rather than soldiers. In a small village like Jinshanling, their official duty is to maintain peace and order. That includes keeping the hawkers at a discreet distance from the tourists. On the other hand, it is legitimate for these hawkers to approach tourists to offer their services as 'helpers', to accompany them during their trek. The pandemonium had resulted from their having rushed forward too fast. You are in China, and negotiations cannot be rushed.

Whatever Alan says, B sees the whole episode in a different light. Some of the hawkers are almost certainly the mothers and aunts of these young soldiers. They are bound to remind their young sons and nephews that nothing gives them the right to order their elders about, and that they will discuss it when they come back home. Both sides have to play out their allotted roles. After a convincing performance, everyone can relax with a clear conscience and enjoy the arrival of tourists with its promise of extra money. B is full of admiration for the way these people, caught in a tug-of-war between official and family duties, find a clever and dignified way not to compromise their harmonious family relationship. She could learn lessons from them.

She rejoices at the thought that she will see her lovely friend Ling again, but must resign herself to the possibility that her idealistic interpretation of Ling's offer of friendship was a little naïve.

Tomorrow we shall discover with her the Jinshanling Great Wall and admire more breathtaking scenery.

7½   Reflections

I must thank you, GM. At last, today felt like the charity challenge I was meant and wanted to join. I can't complain. For a change, you won't have to put up with my reproaches. The accommodation in that mountain village was exactly what I hoped for. On top of that, it made me feel young again. It took me back to the time when I was mountaineering in the Alps and stayed overnight in refuges. Getting up and walking in the dark to that small hut this morning reminded me of walking in the dark on a glacier to approach the rock face of the mountain to be climbed. Don't raise your eyebrows, GM. At my age one needs very little to be transported back from creeping old age to a more exciting time.

Oh dear, why did you make me say that? You know the thought that it will trigger in me. Eric has never been given that chance. From an unacceptably young age his bad knees made sure that he would never have this kind of exciting time. I keep wishing today, as intensely as on the day he was born, that he will experience the same joys I have been given in my life! You're the only one who will never say to me, as they all do to silence me, 'Mother, it's time to cut the umbilical cord. Let Eric rest in peace!" You accept me as I am, GM, hopeless. You are the only one to whom nothing I say is ever a thought to be rid of. I can dump anything on you. You never flinch; you're my unfailing support.

There is no right or wrong way to endure pain, and it remains a daily struggle. As long as we maintain 'mens sana in corpore sano', aren't we all entitled to feel the way we feel, even if we aren't too proud of it? You're the

only one I want to remind me when it's time to give myself a pat on the back.
Where would I be without you? But don't puff yourself up too much with
pride. I owe a lot to Eric, too. I know I can count on his inimitable sense of
humour to keep me safe when the path is treacherous. He has a way to make
me laugh at myself.

An enjoyable time is always enough for me to feel regret. It squeezes my
heart immediately, just as Pilates gives me muscle cramps. Eric is a master
at relieving me of this painful tightening. I remember once, after a
stimulating two-hour discussion with friends in my book club, I felt full of
joy. Yes, I know, here I am, one of those unbearable French 'intellectuals'.
Ha, ha, ha! But let's skip that. You've guessed it, GM, the point of the
anecdote is that I found myself distraught at the thought that Eric would
never have a chance to enjoy such a book club session. Then, I heard him
laughing, 'Not on your life, Maman!' and we both giggled at my ridiculous
thought that he would enjoy discussing books with a group of mature ladies.

You're an attentive and sympathetic listener, GM, even when I rage
against you. But why do you keep me waiting for a few words from you?
All I do is monologue with you, there is no real dialogue. How your silences
can be so calming and disarming is a mystery to me. I would happily let you
speak, and listen to you silently. I see you smiling one of your Sphinx-like
smiles. What do you think I am doing when I am reading my favourite
books, if not listening in silence to their authors? In those books I can hear a
voice that echoes my intimate thoughts, thoughts for which I have no words.
It's soothing to be moved by their words.

Take T.S. Eliot, say. He speaks to me when I read his Quartets. His
visionary lines, 'The intolerable shirt of flame/Which human power cannot
remove', stay with me. You can see why. They make me feel validated when
courage deserts me. In their company, I can deceive myself that they express

my innermost feelings. Words free in me the undying longing to recreate the life that destiny has destroyed, to write the story that has stopped in the middle of a page, unfinished. That might be the way for me to take Eric into a world without 'too late' and 'never again'.

I see you want me to stop getting carried away? All right, back to real life, no more literature. Today was fun. I was asked to be a photographer, I made a lovely new friend, a young Chinese woman. And this morning I woke up early enough to be treated all by myself to a sun rising gloriously above the blushing mountains. This is the view I want to enjoy every day when I am in Paradise. Make a note to yourself about that, GM.

And now I need my beauty sleep. My young friend knows that I am a Naa Naa, I want her to find out tomorrow that I am a young-looking Naa Naa, at least in the morning.

8

The Jinshanling Great Wall at Gubeikou

Once again, B's internal clock wakes her at dawn. By the time her room-mate, recalled from deep sleep, struggles to silence the ringing tone of her alarm, B is fully dressed and ready to leave the room. She steps outside into the small courtyard to enjoy the morning. Wandering on her own beyond its safe perimeter is out of the question. No one gave her Ariadne's thread to unwind through the labyrinth of small alleys when she entered it yesterday evening after the dinner in the restaurant. How could she find her way back today?

It is a glorious morning. The sun is already lapping at one corner of the small courtyard. For a while, she stands immobile inspecting the cloudless blue sky. She could be in California again, where she spent seventeen years bearing her two children and watching their lively games in the constant sunshine. She pushes this fleeting thought aside. There is no room in her mind for the past at this time. To live to the full every minute of the present, to have no past like an amnesiac, no memories to torture her, and no immediate worries for the future, is a blissful relief she deserves. Someone is ensuring that nothing will spoil her Chinese trek.

Soon her room-mate joins her. No getting lost now as they walk briskly through the network of passages between the walled courtyards. Who would know that a young voice inside her is chanting, 'I can't wait to be on the Wall, I can't wait, I can't wait,' her feet dancing to that silent tune? One by one, other members of the group converge on the wide space of the main courtyard at the front of the hotel compound, protected from the outside world by a high brick perimeter wall. Why do the Chinese always want to have walls around them? Is it the need to cocoon themselves, sheltered from the gaze of their neighbours, or is it the desire to exclude them from what they feel is their personal territory? It reminds B of the atavistic instinct demonstrated by very young children playing in a sandbox. Very quickly one of them will draw a line around himself, 'This is my side, don't come in here.' Are they still that child, despite being one of the oldest civilisations in the world?

After the usual breakfast of raw pickled vegetables and eggs, and yet more eggs, that hardly lends itself to narrative, they all gather outside the dining room. B revels in the bracing atmosphere, the light breeze and cool temperature are ideal for walking. Equipped with daypacks of various sizes, walking poles and a few sunhats of different shapes and hues, the group looks quite colourful in the sunshine. Alan checks rapidly that everyone is ready to go and stops near B, whispering to her, 'Another perfect day, B. We are grateful to Eric.' A powerful wave of happiness engulfs her. It washes away the years when she would have gone to the other end of the world to have someone say those words to her. Alan's words will remain with her, safely stored in her treasure chest. Who would have expected her to be with such a sensitive and thoughtful man during this trip? Who made sure that they would meet one day? She feels indebted to a world inhabited by such kind human beings as Alan.

A handful of villagers on the road just outside the front porch, are watching the group silently from a respectful distance. As Alan had explained, they are waiting to be hired as helpers by the Great Wall trekkers. Among them is Ling who waves shyly. B waves back and rushes to shake hands with her. With fractured English and animated gestures, she tries to explain that she does not need her to carry her daypack or to grab her hand to pull her up steep steps. Instead, she wants to have her all day as her private teacher.

A linguist at heart, and a French one at that, B finds it unreasonable to expect the locals always to speak English when she travels abroad. It would be wonderful to acquire a few useful Chinese words while walking. In exchange, she could help Ling expand her limited knowledge of English. What an exciting prospect to be both a student and a teacher. And who knows, when more blood irrigates her ageing grey cells as she climbs up and down the Wall, it might help her to remember these new words for more than a day.

The coach is waiting outside to drive the trekkers back to the outskirts of Gubeikou and drop them at the start of today's hike. Their Chinese helpers are following them packed in a small van. When they arrive there twenty minutes later, and stop alongside the busy road, Alan points to the peaks of the YanShan mountain range that they saw yesterday on each side of the road, Crouching Tiger to the west and Coiling Dragon to the east. What are their names, again, in Chinese, wonders B? She heard them only yesterday. They are stored somewhere in her brain, but alas, the more she struggles to retrieve them, the more she draws a blank. 'Help, Alan. What are they called in Chinese? You told us yesterday, but I can't remember them.'

Alan is always delighted to answer questions about his country. He would have added more to his reply, 'Wohu and Panlong,' if down-to-earth Emma had not cut him short to gather everyone for the inevitable warm-up session. Singing to herself, 'Wohu, Panlong,' B transforms the boring workout into five minutes of invigorating exercises to their rhythm. But will repetition of those two words help her to store them permanently in her memory, as she hopes? Who knows? We had better not test her tomorrow.

At the moment she is champing at the bit while the trekkers and helpers take time to arrange themselves in pairs. Some of the daypacks are passed from British to Chinese shoulders, but B would not dream of letting Ling carry anything for her. At last they set out towards the Panlong Mountain. The path climbs gently but steadily over hill after hill of bare, dry grassland until it reaches a scrap of woodland. When they emerge from it, they find themselves on the crest of the highest hill facing the dilapidated entrance to the Gubeikou Great Wall.

The word 'entrance' is altogether too grand to describe the few bricks piled up to form a small triangular section of Wall on one side of the path, with open land on the other. Alan gathers the Chinese helpers to have them walk together with him past that brick section. As soon as they disappear around it, there is an explosion of voices shouting and arguing at different pitches. The startled group follows quickly through the passage, eager to know what is happening. They discover a very young uniformed guard with a red beret holding a ticket machine and some kind of mobile phone or walkie-talkie. He is standing firmly in front of his screaming countrymen and women. While it is going on, Alan turns towards the group smiling broadly and seemingly amused.

'Don't worry, we'll solve the problem.'

'What problem, Alan? Why are they all shouting at this boy like that? What has he done, or not done, for heaven's sake?'

'Oh, it's just that he is new in the job of gatekeeper and knows only one rule: 'Collect the entrance fee.' So, he wants them to pay the entrance fee, but as they are your allocated helpers, it is free for them on the Wall.'

By now the shouting has ceased. The young guard has learnt the second rule of his job: local helpers do not have to pay the entrance fee. The trekkers and their helpers are at last officially allowed to enter through the gap that he is guarding. They start off again, one behind the other, on the uphill stretch of sandy track that follows the natural line of the hill.

When they reach the next hilltop, it offers a bird's-eye view of impressive mountain scenery that opens up in front of them all the way to the horizon. As far as they can see, the Wall is a sinuous ochre line clinging to the crests of wave after wave of mountains; its regularly-spaced watchtowers like spikes along the back of a sprawling reptile. There are no recently restored Ming brick ramparts streaking the landscape with long lines of bluish grey. The Gubeikou Great Wall reminds B of a discarded necklace with its broken beads still attached to the original but frayed string, a precious object with a fascinating story to tell.

Unlike the imposing Huangyaguan Great Wall, with its brand-new crenellated brick and stone walls, the Gubeikou Great Wall, has been left to show its age. But it is holding its own even in its raw state. Qi Jiguang achieved his ambitious reconstruction plans of facing it with bricks, dotting it with watchtowers resting on huge stone slabs. But that was five centuries ago. Today, dilapidated as it is, supported by this crumpled landscape of mountains and exposed to the immensity of the sky, it acquires an extraordinary grandeur. By exhibiting itself with its scars, its amputations, it tells a magnificent story, the story of an indomitable warrior, wounded, battered, ravaged by the forces of nature, but undefeated.

At this instant, the same sense of a powerful narrative that invaded her mind when she first saw the Great Wall, is again casting its spell on B. To do justice to its monumental presence, and to validate her intuition, she decides that back home, she will study the many chapters of its long history. She will learn more about the strategic role of Gubeikou over the centuries in the defence of Beijing against hordes of nomads from the northern steppes, and more recently against an invading Japanese army. She will discover the fascinating past of this huge structure, and, following the complex phases of this epic history over two millennia, will understand how it was intertwined with the making of a huge Chinese empire.

Each dynasty of the Middle Kingdom, after it was unified by the First Emperor, had to deal with the fundamental problem of the northern frontier. It was claimed as essential by the agrarian Chinese settlers to protect their position as guardians of the greatest civilisation. For the nomads from the Mongolian steppes, unfairly despised as barbarians and evil spirits, it represented an access route to trade their livestock and furs in exchange for Chinese farm produce and silk. Under certain warlike Emperors the colossal task of Wall-building was the chosen solution to prevent raids and pillage, but it required a huge workforce of army and civilian labour, and it drained the financial resources of the empire.

Other Emperors were opposed to the exclusion of the nomads by a Wall and preferred an open-door policy. They advocated trade and diplomacy, including gifts of their daughters. They succeeded in negotiating peaceful coexistence that lasted for years during certain dynasties. Often, however, inefficiency and corruption of the court officials, and nepotism in the dynasty system, led the Emperor to take wrong decisions for the wrong reasons. Whatever the fluctuations in Great Wall politics, they rarely resolved satisfactorily the frontier conflicts.

The Ming dynasty fell in 1644 when the nomadic Manchus invaded the Middle Kingdom, and established in Beijing the Qing dynasty that ruled over China until 1911. Wall building stopped, as there was no longer any need to protect the northern frontier. When that last dynasty was brought down in 1911, and the new Republic of China was declared a year later, its first President, Sun Yat-sen, understood well the symbolic role that the Great Wall could play. But it took Chairman Mao many turbulent years to reach the same conclusion. At first, he had self-interested reasons to revile the ancient Wall, as evidence of the workforce having been exploited by the despotic First Emperor, Qin Shi Huang. He gave it to the people to tear to pieces, as pagan tyrants threw Christians to the lions. But in later years, he represented it as solid proof of what the strength and endurance of the masses had been able to achieve, and declared it a symbol of the great Chinese nation. In one of his poems he proclaims, 'He who has never been to the Great Wall is not a true man; and he who does not love the Great Wall is not a hero.' In today's People's Republic of China, the Great Wall is the centre of a patriotic cult and contributes to China's great-power status in the world.

But let us go back to the time when B is striding along the Wall. Through her decision to learn more in depth about the Great Wall's relation with the Chinese past, she realises that by hiking on it, following its every twist and turn, she is creating a personal link with its history. Something tells her that she needs to experience its physicality to be able to commune spiritually with it, to feel it with her feet, and with every fibre of her body. This trek is a unique chance to apprehend the Great Wall with all her senses, almost to absorb its presence into herself.

These ten days in the YanShan mountains are a fantastic voyage of discovery. And they are also a special treat for B. Since her childhood, a mysterious energy flows into her whenever she is climbing uphill, or even upstairs. And she is rejoicing at the prospect of today's seven-hour trek, first on the Gubeikou Great Wall and then on the Jinshanling Great Wall.

Walking on the rising and falling hills, following the track that leads from one watchtower to the next, is prime terrain for a robust rambler like her. There is not a cloud in the sky. The low sun is beginning to light up the Wall, adding a golden glow to its stones. She feels the familiar joy of breathing the invigorating mountain air, of listening to the silence, of being in touch with the splendour of a glorious landscape. This morning, she is in the mood to climb anything, everything, all the way to the sky. Why? She could not say, but it is real.

Ling discovers to her surprise that she has to run to catch up with her elderly client who sets off briskly on the path zooming up to the first watchtower. That tower has lost its roof and parts of its walls, and it is so unsafe that the entrance has been filled with stones to prevent people from getting inside. There is no other choice than to leave the Wall, to walk on the track around it, and then to rejoin the Wall on the other side.

Further on, the slope flattens off slightly. On the gently undulating terrain, the Wall cannot take advantage of natural mountain ridges and steep slopes that make it unscalable. It has to rise high above ground. Here it runs on top of a man-made platform of rammed earth, buttressed by stone-faced retaining walls, eight to ten metres high. It has lost the paved walkway and the brick parapets that originally capped it. But, despite its elevation and the absence of parapets, it is safe to walk on it, as it is a couple of metres wide and not very steep. Its sandy surface, invaded by tussocks of dry grass and grey-brown brush, is unkempt and wild.

Struggling vegetation clinging to the barren foothills looks exhausted and parched. Rain seems desperately needed. The only suggestions of spring arriving soon are the white powder puffs of the sparse fruit trees in full blossom dotted randomly on the slopes. They provide a welcome touch of colour against a dull canvas of scrub.

Higher up, the Wall takes a sudden twist at the edge of a small plateau. From there, the view opens up again onto a splendid expanse of mountains with the uninterrupted ribbon of the Wall, studded with towers, clinging to the highest ridges. It provides an ideal lookout to spot an advancing enemy, and indeed a watchtower once stood there. But over the centuries, wind and rain have got the better of it. All that is left is the few large slabs of stone that paved the area where the ground floor was. It looks as if flattened by a bomb, with rough stones scattered around, some ready to tumble down the slope below.

For another kilometre, what was originally designed to provide a strategic tower-to-tower walkway is mostly a series of zigzags around vestiges and empty shells on a trail running beside the Wall. It seems a miracle when they finally arrive at a mostly intact large tower, isolated at the top of a steep hill. From below it looks like a cube-shaped two-storey construction, precariously planted across the Wall at a point where it twists sharply and changes direction. A steep ramp climbs up to the arched doorway of its upper floor. The northern and southern façades have openings that let daylight into the central corridor leading to the next section of the Wall on the other side.

This will make a great picture. The walking boots stop walking, the cameras start clicking, and one hears Emma, as always the decisive tour leader, declaring, 'We must have a group photo here with all of you and your helpers. It will look good in your scrapbooks and in the NewShores brochure.' Everyone scrambles up the ramp in front of the entrance to the tower and stands to attention while Alan volunteers to take the picture.

B suddenly realises that she has not exchanged one word with Ling until now. She hurries to her and greets her with a few welcoming 'Hellos.' How could she explain to this young woman why she appears to have ignored her? How could she explain it in Chinese? Or in any language? How could she say that this breathtaking landscape takes her to a world where she has no longer the sense of who she is, what she wants, or where she is going. In that disconnected space there are no longer words or thoughts that bind her to the vagaries of life, no situation that she cannot escape. Everything is free, endless, silent. The beauty of the mountains, to be able to embrace it, to measure her own smallness against the vast expanse of earth and sky, that ecstasy is a source of strength and joy for her alone. It cannot be shared.

Reluctantly, she emerges from that inner world to rejoin the human race, to be again one of the fourteen volunteers on that fundraising trip. She turns towards Ling and asks, 'You are my teacher, Ling. How do you say 'beautiful' in Chinese?' It is hard for B to believe that she can count on this young villager to teach her the right words. Imagine what reply a Chinese tourist hiking in the English countryside would receive from a farmer's daughter if she asked her that kind of question? She is grateful when Ling answers without hesitation, 'Piao liang.' Unfortunately, when she begins to repeat the word, trying to use the right tones helped by her young coach, she is cut short by Alan who has come out of the watchtower. and stands by its entrance. Spotlit by the morning sun, and framed by the arched doorway, he reminds B of the statues that adorn the portal of Chartres Cathedral. His sense of theatre always leads him to choose the best platform to make a grand entrance and address his audience.

'Today we are walking on the Gubeikou Wall and later the Jinshanling Wall. The Gubeikou pass was the best access point into Beijing for the nomads and it saw many battles. Even against Japanese invaders in 1938. The great Ming general-architect, Qi Jiguang, had to repair and rebuild existing sixth-century sections of the Wall and to add new ones to create a solid line of defence. Unlike the Huangyaguan Great Wall, it has not been restored recently and its brick parapets are in poor condition. But something has survived here that says 'Ming Wall'. What do you think it is?'

Here, Alan pauses and looks expectantly at the faces turned towards him. He is enjoying his professorial role, forgetting that his audience is not sitting in a classroom, and not keen to be tested when on holiday. Is B going to show off? She cannot remain silent like the rest of the group. It is not a game of Trivial Pursuit. Her imagination is taking her back to the time when Qi Jiguang had to fight the Emperor and court officials to impose his grand design. 'Do you mean the watchtowers, Alan? We have never seen so many. They are on every mountain ridge here, all the way to the horizon. It's incredible. Have you ever attempted to count how many we can see from here?'

'Some guidebooks say there are over a hundred from Gubeikou to Jinshanling. Qi Jiguang was a tactical genius. He designed a remarkable network of defences with watchtowers integrated into the Wall, according to the risks of invasion presented by the terrain. It allowed easy access for the soldiers to run in either direction as needed, it offered strategic points to take aim at the approaching attackers, and protection from the elements. What's important is to understand the various functions of these towers. You have the watchtowers on the Wall itself. They vary in size and shape. Some garrison towers can accommodate up to fifty soldiers. And you have the beacon towers on the slopes where they can be seen from the Wall and the garrison towers. They relayed signals from tower to tower, by way of fires at night or smoke by day, and alerted the garrisons to advancing enemies. The archaeologist, Aurel Stein, called it 'optic telegraphy'.

'We are going through this tower now, but further on we walk downwards on a path next to a section of Wall that is being used by the military authorities. We're not allowed to stop anywhere along the wired enclosure, nor to take pictures '

It is the first time that Alan has mentioned that kind of interdiction and he looks ill at ease. Such restrictions suggest a police state rather than the positive image of his country that he wants to convey. Luckily, no one is keen to question him and embarrass him even more.

A queue forms at the tower entrance. Everyone, camera at the ready, wants to stop inside. Through the gaping holes on each side of the internal corridor, they enjoy a grandstand view of ripples of mountains topped by the Great Wall. It is essential to select the best field of view and to take striking pictures framed by the jagged edge of one of the arched windows in the tower's northern side. For some, it is what makes such a trek worthwhile.

Further on, past the military zone, the path leads the group down to the valley. On a narrow country lane they come across an old shepherd leading a few goats. He is only the second person they have met on their walks so far. He would look splendid in a picture, but he is camera-shy and as soon as B grabs hers he raises his stick. Immediately, she wishes that she knew how to apologise to him in Chinese for her lack of respect. What gives her the right to intrude into the life of this decent man? She must control her impetuosity. Her eagerness to record every minute of this trip is no excuse for this kind of behaviour.

After a rapid picnic on a patch of grassland, it is time to move on. They walk for a short while on a country road past a few dilapidated farmhouses, seeing in front of each the now familiar stack of government bricks beside a half-built wall.

Soon they begin to climb across fields towards the top of a wooded hill. A small heap of earth, twice as high as a molehill and with a regular conical shape sticks out in the middle of one of the fields. Alan stops and points to it. 'This is a burial mound. It is built by the farmer who owns the field and it contains the ashes of his ancestors. It belongs to this patch of earth that generations of his family have cultivated. Ancestors are venerated in China. At least until now. But young people today don't respect our fundamental values. Sadly, they admire only American ways.'

While Alan is talking, the group has gathered silently around the small tumulus, but this time not to take pictures. A reflective mood prevails with everyone lost in their own thoughts. Even if only briefly, the quiet despair inherent in the human condition can readily invade the mind, though the longing to escape it is the same for all. In such moments, the world is reduced to the spot where you stand. You are a mere fragment of the human race; differences in life experiences, culture and colour are effaced.

Higher up the slope, the group asks to rest briefly in the shade under the trees. How wrong and inexperienced they are. B has to remain standing and jogging slowly around them. If her ageing leg muscles, tendons and ligaments were allowed to cool down in the middle of the walk, they would refuse to get back into action without inflicting pain. When the temperature is low, you have to keep the engine running with old cars. To prove her point, when Alan starts walking briskly again, she is the only one able to keep pace with him. They leave the group behind dragging their feet and panting.

When they come out of the shadowy forest and reach the edge of the plateau, B is the first of the group to be rewarded with the breathtaking view that opens out before her. The Jinshanling Wall stretches all the way to the horizon, like a long string linking its closely-spaced watchtowers. They stand defiantly, silhouetted against the bright blue sky. It is as if this continuous line, glowing golden yellow in the early afternoon sunshine, is crowning the mountains. Her gaze follows its twists and turns, as it rises up and down the crest of wave after wave before disappearing into the distance. Without thinking, standing there in awe, she opens her arms wide, tilts her face towards the sky and exclaims at the top of her voice, 'Piao liang, piao liang!' Alan is watching her in silence, smiling his Sphinx-like smile. She turns towards him and repeats softly, 'Piao liang.' At that moment she knows that her spontaneous outburst has happened in front of the only witness able to understand the reason for it. Everything in the world is as it should be.

The rest of the group have now joined them, and it is time to stride downhill to reach the Wall's rampart and to find the nearest opening to gain access to that formidable Jinshanling Great Wall. As soon as she stands on its walkway, B cannot say why, but a feeling of gratitude buoys her up. Gratitude towards that seven-hundred-year-old stone colossus for permitting her to see how it has survived. Gratitude for the immense empathy that she feels with this glorious warrior, never succumbing in spite of the injuries inflicted by the forces of nature. Gratitude for being overwhelmed by its powerful presence, for being humbled by its grandeur. Piao liang!

She turns towards Ling who has been shadowing her all morning. 'Oh Ling, your Great Wall is so beautiful! Piao liang. I am so happy to be here. So happy! What is 'happy' in Chinese?' As expected, Ling has to say the word a few times before B is able to figure out how to repeat it with some sort of Chinese intonation. 'Gaoxìng?...Yes?... Gaoxing!' Ling giggles joyously, pressing her small fist against her mouth. B would love to shout 'piao liang, gaoxing' and let the words echo from tower to tower breaking the silence of the mountains. Even though the Newshores group and their helpers are the only people on the Wall today, she decides to refrain from such impulsive behaviour. The silence should remain unbroken.

After many years in Britain, she has learnt not to let strong emotions make her annoyingly voluble and loud. During the two days following Eric's death, she always waited for the house to be empty before wailing incoherently until her vocal chords cried out for mercy. Fortunately, brisk walking is another useful way for her to channel her emotions. And, just at the right time, a massive watchtower seems to be challenging her to scramble up the slope leading to its entrance. She arrives swiftly and out of breath at its jagged doorway and walks inside, as resolute as the Mongol invaders who might have stormed it centuries ago. What fun it is to re-enact in the safety of her mind such bloody events. She smiles at the thought of her pretty four-year-old granddaughter whose favourite pastime is to play at being Batman or Darth Vader. She imagines already how much prestige she will acquire in her eyes when she describes to her the warlike games she could have played on the Chinese Great Wall.

No one in the group can resist the urge to take a picture of the stunning ocean of mountains within their field of view through the arched doorway. It is the ideal vantage point, offering both the scenery and the unusual frame of the jaggedly damaged entrance. At this time of day, the light picks out the sharp edges of the rough stones and creates a dramatic contrast. B wishes she could stay for more than the few minutes allowed to the group. How she would like to come back for a whole day alone, encased in the thick walls of this tower, contemplating the splendid décor in the ever-changing light.

The next tower is square; its top platform has lost its crenellation and its arrow slits for soldiers to shoot at the enemy. It is reduced to flattened stonework with tufts of grass growing out of it. On one side, it is pockmarked with holes that Alan explains were made by Japanese bullets during the nineteen-thirties. Ahead of her, B can see a string of watchtowers along the rampart at no more than hundred-metre intervals. They all vary in size, in shape and in the degree of damage they have suffered. What remains of the Wall is a wide and even path at the top of the high rampart. There are no narrow vertiginous stretches that force her to concentrate on where she places her feet. Her gaze sweeps across the vast scenery, following unbroken lines of Great Wall, some sections meandering off in puzzling directions.

The inclines between towers are no more strenuous than those she used to climb during her walking holidays in Italy or Spain with her husband. She has no desire to climb faster, to steal a march on the group, but only a fast pace feels comfortable to her. She is striding effortlessly with a spring in her step. She feels weightless. She could walk for ever.

Her faithful companion, The Wall, shows her the way. It is climbing up and down the mountain ridges in front of her, behind her, twisting and turning at right angles, clinging to the contours of the mountains. The sunlight penetrates the openings on the sides of the watchtowers and sets them ablaze. She gazes enraptured at this surreal spectacle. She is floating in a bubble of happiness. '*Verweile doch! Du bist so schön!*'

Suddenly she crumples on the Great Wall path, a sobbing heap clinging to the ground, powerful and invisible forces are shaking her. Powerful waves of grief have beaten her to the ground. Her Erynies swirl around her. She chokes on words she cannot speak. She is drowning in a maelstrom of longing, regrets, self-hate. Around her, the glorious mountains, the radiant sky, wait patiently, tenderly conspiring to shelter her.

After a time that cannot be measured in human terms, she regains control of the muscles in her shoulders. She licks the last salty tears off her face. She jumps to her feet, shakes her legs, stretches her arms, gulps avidly the brisk mountain air. Nothing pulls and tugs at her heart any more, she can breathe freely again. She smiles at Jimmy who has stayed next to her. As the tour GP, he always walks at the rear of the group. She apologises and explains that such a spell of uncontrollable sobbing has not happened for many years since Eric's death. It has taken her entirely by surprise today. She reassures him that they always bring her profound relief, and that she is absolutely fine now.

Jimmy's sympathetic reaction feels genuine, and more personal than the bedside manners GPs are taught at medical school. 'OK, B, let's have a picture of both of us smiling. It'll be a good memory for you, and for Eric. He doesn't want you to be unhappy. Never forget that.' He waves at Ling, who has remained close by, puzzled by the whole episode. B hands her camera to her.

For the next half-hour the trio stride on the rampart path taking them further up and down the mountain. They are chatting, laughing, joking. Such happiness is exhilarating and needs to be celebrated. B stops suddenly and with both hands opened around her mouth like a megaphone, she shouts, 'Piao liang, Gaoxing,' facing in turns the east, the south, the west and the north. She needs to surround herself with the magical echo of these two newly acquired Chinese words. A few moments later they see the rest of the group assembled down below on a wide stone platform, built recently over the remains of a ruined watchtower.

When they are all together, and Alan is preparing to take the group through the opening in the parapet that leads onto the track down to the village, he turns around, comes to B and clasps her in his arms. He whispers into her ear, 'B, I want to write something in the picture book on the Great Wall you bought yesterday. I'll write it in Chinese.' 'Thank you, Alan, what are you going to write?' 'I'll write, "He Is Still Here".'

Now, the group is gathering to follow Alan down to the valley. But where is B? Let us leave her floating in a bubble of joy that ought never to burst.

8½   **Reflections**

Why didn't you take hold of me today, GM, when I tumbled into that Eric-shaped hole again? You don't scold or cajole, but can't you show pity? All you want is to test me, to show my mettle, knowing that I shall fail miserably. I collapsed, so are you satisfied? Oh, yes, you are always there, but what good does that do? I struggled on my own in the torrent where I search for Eric.

Why, why, did you bring me to this magical place? I never suspected that its natural and man-made splendours would cast such a spell on me. I never suspected that it would make me feel alive again, happy and eager to enjoy every minute of the day. That hurts, and I don't want to suffer like that.

You tricked me. You lured me to China under the false pretences of supporting a worthy cause. You knew that it was going to expose me to torturing thoughts. You knew my tormentors. You knew the questions that rage inside me. Why am I walking on that stunning Great Wall in that sublime landscape? Why am I walking effortlessly and free of pain at my age? Why was such a chance denied to Eric when he was more than half a century younger than I am?

I don't have the key that might make sense of it all. I don't even believe that such a key exists. We are no more than a pair of lungs inhaling and exhaling for a brief period, and then they stop, for no good reason. That's all. Absurdity rules our lives and the world.

Even more absurd, GM, is that you are here, next to me, and you make me soliloquise before you. I have to put up with your cruel silence. Am I talking nonsense? Well, that's how it may sound to you. But if it does, why are you staying with me? Are you simply too polite to leave me? How come that you let me go on and on, ranting, and accusing? You even seem to encourage me to keep talking when you nod and smile just at the right moments. You know, GM, having you there, always ready to listen to me, actually makes me feel a little bit better. You're a fine psychiatrist. And you don't charge anything.

Shall I tell you about a real psychiatrist? The only one who ever used the right tactics with me. When I explained that I had to cope with regrets, remorse, feelings of guilt, since Eric's death, he didn't ask why, or reply that I shouldn't. He said, 'B, when one is guilty, what happens? One gets punished, and doesn't do it again.' I can't tell you how many times, the logic of his answer has had a miraculous effect on me. Losing Eric is how I got punished, and I don't do it again quite obviously. His few words never fail to work their chemistry on me. They relieve instantly the stinging acidity of my inner thoughts, as acid plus base makes soothing salt plus water. In my eyes, that psychiatrist deserves his excellent reputation; he is the best.

What I try to forget, though, is what he said years later, when I thanked him for the extraordinary effect that his words have on me, again and again. His casual reply was, 'Oh, you know B, we are not always sure what to say to patients, so we just say whatever comes into our heads.' Did he want to undermine my confidence in him? He failed. He made me laugh then, and I can see, GM, that you're giggling too. For the first time I've caught you by surprise. At last, you've lost your reserve. My first win against you, you've made my day!

Having you react like that gives me the strength to follow on with my train of thought. You see, GM, fifty years ago I had nine hours a week of

117

philosophy in my last Baccalaureate year at the Lycée. Existentialism was high fashion in France. Camus was my pop idol, and still is. I worshipped his 'absurd hero', Sisyphus. It helps me to think of myself as carrying a heavy stone and, like Sisyphus, without feeling sorry for myself. You've never heard me, and will never hear me, complaining about the weight of grief I have to carry day after day. It is my uphill struggle. I've never said, 'Why me?' I've always said, 'Why Eric?' From the moment I heard of his death, I have asked, and will always ask, 'Why Eric?' I can't say, like Pope after Homer, 'Who dies in youth and vigour dies the best.'

I can't complain. I have known many of the joys of adult life, my suffering is part of its sorrows. But Eric has never known, and will never know, the joys of adult life. His death makes no sense. I'll never reconcile myself to the fact that life was cut short for him, so young.

I wish I could accept Camus' last words in his Myth of Sisyphus. 'The struggle itself towards the heights is enough to fill a man's heart. One must imagine Sisyphus happy.' I can't carry my stone so lightly, I'm weak, I stumble with it. The struggle towards the heights often chokes my heart, like today. I'm certainly not a happy Sisyphus, but I'm not a complaining one.

GM, your efforts to hide your yawns are laudable, but unsuccessful. Here I am, an insufferably pretentious bore, regurgitating half-digested philosophy, babbling away like a French intellectual. I know, but in an odd way, it helps me. When I struggle in the torrent where I search for Eric, you leave me on my own. Why don't you at least make more of an effort to listen to me?

If you had concentrated, you would have detected what I did not say! You would have noticed that I don't follow my guru Camus, when he concludes that rolling the stone uphill is a way to 'negate the gods.' If I believed that, I wouldn't see the point of talking to you, I would keep myself to myself. Why would I still hope to force you to answer my questions, to break your silence? I am convinced that you have an important role to play in my life, even if I can't see what it is yet. But beware, I might give up on you if you make me wait too long.

Don't you think it's time I ended my sermon, GM? I do. After all, you are not that bad as a walking companion. I can't expect Eric, my other faithful companion on that fantastic Grande Muraille de Chine, to listen to his mother as patiently as you do. He debated brilliantly in his A-level philosophy class. No comparison with my feeble reasoning. His pop idol was Nietzsche. Right now I wish he would quote him to make fun of me, 'All truly great thoughts are conceived by walking,' and we would both burst out laughing. I miss hearing him laugh.

How is it that a kind Chinese could find wonderful words to whisper to me and you can't? They will be forever engraved on my heart. He is still here.

9

The Jinshanling Great Wall - North

The sun is preparing to rise in a cloud-free sky when B wakes up. What an encouraging sign for her second and final day in Jinshanling. The advantage of travelling light is that, after the agony of deciding what to remove from her luggage before leaving home, she is now able to pack in record time. She is soon pulling her suitcase along the narrow alleys and joins the group in the dining room well ahead of her room-mate. The four previous walks have strengthened her legs and increased her stamina - as if she needed more of it! No need today to take any medicine for sore muscles. She is ready, even eager, to meet the seven-hour challenge to the next destination.

While she is enjoying a leisurely breakfast, sipping her cup of instant coffee, she notices that most of the group are standing around a table in the far corner. What are they doing holding photo albums of the Great Wall and handing them to Alan sitting at that table? Of course! He is autographing them. How could she forget to bring hers? She rushes outside to grab her pack before the coach driver has had time to load it on the coach, and takes out her book. When she presents it to Alan, he looks at her and asks her to open it at her favourite view of the Wall. Every stroke of his pen writing the Chinese characters on the page is like a familiar sound. They whisper to her the words, 'He Is Still Here,' and she hears them in her heart, in a language that is neither Chinese, nor English, nor French; a language that needs no translation. When he hands her the book, she examines the line of beautiful calligraphy with the same fervour as if she were reading her personal Book of Hours. The precious gift goes back into her daypack. She will carry it with her for the rest of her trek on the Great Wall.

Through the large bay windows of the restaurant, she can see the local helpers who accompanied the group yesterday. They are waiting on the road by the entrance, hoping to be of service. Once again, B admires their restraint. If she were as poor as they are, she would have rushed inside the guest house courtyard and attached herself to her customer from the previous walk to secure a few extra coins.

After the familiar warm-up routine with Emma, and the essential tour of inspection by Alan, everyone is ready to go. They walk through the gate to the road and exchange cheerful greetings with the waiting Chinese. Just as they start moving on, B opens her camera and turns to take a last picture of the sign 'Jinshan Hotel' posted on one of the pillars at the entrance, just beneath the usual row of plump and welcoming red lanterns. But, who is standing behind her? The five young soldier-policemen who dutifully protected the group from local hawkers when they stepped out of the coach on their arrival two days ago. B instantly feels her maternal heart melting. They look so serious under their stiff regulation caps, and they are so young and so touching in their khaki uniforms too big for them.

Deliberately ignoring the others' vehement advice, 'No, B, you can't take a picture of them, you'll be in trouble, they might rip out the film and destroy it,' she waves her camera, smiling engagingly. She points an interrogating finger at the young men, while opening her eyes wide and emitting a few imploring 'Hm, hm, hmhmhm?' Four of them immediately form a straight line, standing to attention and beaming with pride to have been selected for the great honour of being immortalised. Click, click, they are now on film, below the red lanterns and between the crouching stone lions flanking the entrance pillars

But where is number five? At that moment, B feels like Snow White caring for her seven dwarfs. She looks around and finds him standing bashfully just behind her. Without hesitation this time, she grabs him by his sleeve, drags him next to the line of four and gesticulates to warn him not to run away. When she looks again at the scene through the viewfinder of her camera, to check their position in the frame, she realises that the line of five has become a line of six. Yes, six men, all of them laughing. The sixth one is none other than the uninvited burly coach driver in dark navy clothing standing tall above the others, his arms crossed defiantly and with a big smile on his moonlike face.

By that time, the timorous British group has found the courage to come back, eager now to take pictures of the scene. Everyone relishes being part of what has become a friendly and exciting game. In a sense, by adding players, it is a reversal of the western game of musical chairs. As for B shaking with laughter, she can hardly believe how good it feels to be allowed to live again moments of pure childish fun.

If only she were using a digital camera, she could show these young men how splendid they look on the small screen. But it was her choice not to purchase one before leaving for China. Years ago, she had lent her new camera to Eric when he went as a twelve-year-old pupil on a cruise to Egypt with his prep school. She had half expected him to damage or lose it. Instead he had brought back stunning pictures and an intact camera. Ever since, she carries it on all her trips as a precious talisman.

How can she communicate her appreciation to these young men in the absence of visual aids, and despite the language barrier? With her hands, of course; she is French, remember. She raises her closed right hand with her thumb erect, a typically

British gesture borrowed from the Romans that her women friends, and even her husband, find vulgar and would never make. This is a first for her, too. Later on during the day, it will dawn on her that it might actually have sent a very confusing, possibly improper, message to these Chinese villagers. Such are the hazards of cross-culture and cross-continents.

Over the coming years, each time she looks at the printed photos of the whole episode, she will laugh at herself and remember it fondly. Only then will she realise that it was also another first for her. At that moment, she had been able to mix with young men on the threshold of adulthood, like Eric, without feeling a sharp pang of pain. It had never been so during the previous thirteen years.

Having waved goodbye to Jinshan Hotel and the small squadron protecting it, the NewShores group is now on its way to the northern section of Jinshanling Great Wall. They follow the perimeter wall of the hotel complex for a few hundred metres and find themselves on a country lane in the direction of the hilltop. They pass a few low dwellings, some hidden at the back of their enclosed courtyards, others directly beside the lane. Their facades, a mixture of bricks and timber powdered with dry dust, have lost their original colour and can only be described as nondescript. The same pale dust is everywhere, uniformly spread on the path, and even clinging to the clothing of the few villagers who are already outdoors.

It would be easy to assume that life in that small village could only be as dull as this colourless countryside. However, the day before, Ling, her young Chinese helper had explained in her limited English that in China several generations live under the same roof. In her own case, she has to share a house with her husband, his mother and a few married siblings with children.

In B's western mind, given the number of ingredients combined in such cramped accommodation, it could hardly be a recipe for a bland or even peaceful life.

At the moment, the young adults, either already away at work somewhere, or too busy with indoor chores, are nowhere to be seen. The village appears to be inhabited only by people bowed down by the weight of advanced age, walking slowly back and forth along the length of their houses, and a few small children milling aimlessly around them. All the faces are either completely shrivelled up, like windfall plums left on the ground, or deliciously plump and smooth. At last, one dwelling in the village offers a scene that, in B's eyes, merits immediate action with her camera. A very young boy crouching on the front steps of a small house, and another one, who could be his twin, perched precariously above him on a narrow window sill, are watching her approaching with no sign of being frightened or even puzzled by her. Charmingly, they decide to wave with a timid 'Hello' in response to B's enthusiastic greetings and gesticulations. More 'Hellos' are exchanged, quickly followed by 'Bye-byes,' for as long as she walks backwards to keep waving at the pair, until she catches up with the rest of the group.

Back in England, she will look at the printed picture with those fresh-faced boys and notice that, even if their features are undoubtedly Chinese, their baseball caps, their baggy trousers and padded jackets, their sneakers, are similar to those worn by every boy in the western world. What is strikingly different is the house in front of which they are sitting. It is of a sort that she had not seen before. Its two windows and the upper part of its double front door are of intricate latticework. Their openwork, made of assembled wooden strips that form geometric patterns, is backed by what appears to be a tobacco-stained sheet of glass with only a few clean patches at eye level, or which could actually be flat panels of some sort of sepia-tinted material.

She will learn that intricate latticework on doors and windows, China's traditional ornamentation, is mainly a legacy of the Ming dynasty. This distinct artistic style prevails, with various patterns and motifs, on all the palaces reserved for Emperors and their high-ranking entourages, and is still applied today on expensive modern buildings. But who would have the time and money in this remote village to build a house that follows the artistic traditions of his country? She will never know.

Beyond the village, the lane narrows and becomes a winding path through leafless bushes and small trees climbing the slope towards the Great Wall. Despite the incline, B accelerates, as if obeying a pressing desire to distance herself from her chatting and laughing companions. Adopting such a pace answers a need to detach herself from any cheerful group, and to rejoin the invisible crowd of those whose life is a painful struggle. At that point, she is no longer a twenty-first century westerner. She is time-travelling back to the Ming period when Wall building had resumed frantically under the direction of architect-in-chief Qi Jiguang. She is walking among conscripted peasants and soldiers, drafted unwillingly into the construction of the Wall.

Instead of the light daypack on her back, she is carrying one of their heavy stone slabs. She feels that being very fit, and finding the incline no real challenge for her, is somehow reprehensible. Like them, she should be struggling to ascend and needing to pause for breath. She should be feeling their fatigue, and waiting anxiously for the moment when she too would be allowed to deposit her load.

Today again, China is casting its spell on her. In this brief moment of fusion between past and present, she is able to join ranks with the human race again. She feels no more disconnected and alone, no more a lost dot on the line of time. But how long can the luxury of such a comforting illusion last? Raising her eyes towards the cloudless sky in an instinctive gesture of gratitude, she catches sight of a couple of red oversized metal lanterns dangling from a cable above her head. For a few seconds, her mind refuses to recognize them as cable car cabins. Such an anachronism in her field of vision irritates her. The twenty-first century has no right to intrude and destroy the magic.

In fact, the village that their group has just left has been dreaming of moving into the twenty-first century. This ultra-modern cable car is part of their planning for a golden future when their section of the Great Wall attracts hordes of tourists. There will soon be a booming economy with the vulgar trappings of western attractions. These red cabins will disgorge unfit and undiscerning visitors onto this magnificent Jinshanling Wall. A profusion of T-shirts and postcards will be sold, empty Coca-Cola bottles will be scattered around. Fortunately, the cable car is out of action at the moment. At the bottom of a large panel covered in Chinese characters hanging above the door of its station it says in big letters, 'The Jinshan cableway is repairing.'

A quick reassessment brings B back to her senses. She feels ashamed to be secretly pleased by this breakdown of a much-needed source of revenue in a country where people are desperate to improve their lot. In less than a week, she will be going back to her comfortable and secure English life, enriched by memories of her Chinese experiences, but for these villagers their harsh existence will continue. A sudden thought crosses her mind. She must encourage her friends in England to see this stunning Great Wall as quickly as possible, before it has degenerated into a garish tourist trap.

After half an hour on the path, the group reaches the brow of the hill and steps onto the large paved platform where they had arrived the day before at the end of their walk on the southern section of the Jinshanling Wall. A few women hawkers are already there. One of them extracts a small blanket from a tattered cardboard box at her feet. She unfolds it fully to reveal in each of its six sections a family of black and white pandas rolling around on a white background as fluffy as snow. It works like a red cape waved in front of a bull. The group surges around her.

Only B can resist the attraction of hugging these baby pandas and securing a bargain. Standing on the platform away from the hawkers, she welcomes the few minutes she has to herself. Will she again today enter another world and escape from the one in which she has been living for years? She lets her eyes sweep slowly over the wide expanse in front of her and does not attempt to take it all in. She is alone in the middle of an ocean of hills and mountain ranges crested by the Great Wall, sunning itself like an immense octopus, its tentacles stretched out in several directions, soaring and plunging with every undulation of the waves. Transfixed, succumbing once again to the power of that massive monument, so present, so permanent, so reassuring, she remains motionless wishing this moment taken out of time could last for ever.

A loud, 'Hey, you guys, it's time to move on,' puts an abrupt end to her reverie and jolts her back to reality. At the other end of the platform, Alan who has waited philosophically to resume his role of tour guide, and to take them on today's walk, is now ready to go. It is typical of him to adopt the easy familiarity of American slang while keeping his Chinese accent and respectful reserve. A difficult balance, but he is an excellent acrobat.

Much agitation follows. Soon a line of docile walkers forms behind him. As always, B is eager to start, exhilarated by the idea that her feet will again cover a long stretch of the Great Wall that was built by bare hands centuries ago. If only she knew how to convey her sense of excitement to the others. Perhaps some of them would understand why she is fretting like a racehorse before galloping away when the gate is lifted.

Starting where they left off the previous day, they climb up a few restored steps of the Jinshanling Great Wall, this time heading north towards Simatai. At the top, they begin to ascend a stone-paved, six-metre-wide corridor, walled on both sides by crenellated brick parapets. It rises towards a three-storied watchtower high above them. On the left half of the walkway, is a succession of some ten walls a few steps apart, at right angles to the parapet.

Alan stops the group to explain. 'You see these half walls facing you on the left side of the steps, they are called 'obstacle walls'. They are unique to the Jinshanling Great Wall. Do you know why they have a hole at eye level? Well, sometimes the nomads managed to climb over the parapets of the Great Wall. Soldiers garrisoned in the watchtower had to come out quickly and take up positions behind these obstacle walls to repel the attack. The holes are for shooting at the assailants.'

'What use were the watchtowers, then?' someone asks.

When acting as a tour guide, Alan's serious personality takes over. Now is an occasion to instruct the group and he seizes it.

'In the watchtower, food and weapons were stored on the ground floor. The upper floor served to accommodate the troops. The crenellated platform on top was used both as a lookout and for fighting off Mongol raids. Often, there was no stairway. The soldiers must have climbed up retractable ladders or ropes through an opening in the ceiling to retreat to the upper floor. That was to prevent attackers who had managed to scale the Great Wall parapets from reaching the soldiers in their living quarters. The attackers were then easy targets from above.

'The defending soldiers were frequently unpaid for months, when corrupt officials stole the funds intended for their pay. They were often starved and badly equipped, and in no shape to perform their watch duties. Sometimes the small openings at the base of the parapets for rainwater to run off were used to trade their weapons for food from the attackers. Their situation was inhuman. Morale of both officers and men was low, and some deserted.'

Alan's moving comments seem to have induced a reflective mood in the group. They resume their ascent past the obstacle walls in silence and scramble to enter the tower. It is still early morning, but the air feels warm in the bright sunshine. By contrast, entering the ground floor of the watchtower is like entering the chilly atmosphere of a tomb. The eyes need time to get used to the darkness, to make out the inner walls dividing the space into six narrow areas, communicating with each other. The light that penetrates through the arched openings in the exterior walls is insufficient to dispel the gloom.

It is hard to believe that ten to fifty soldiers had to share the harsh grey realities of life in this gloomy bunker, through freezing winters and sizzling summers. Their only fuel was cow or wolf dung, and they had to wait for farm produce to be brought from the valleys by their families. Boredom must have been their most insidious enemy.

When B looks out through a window, she can hardly control a shudder, caused not by the cold atmosphere inside the watchtower but by her imagination running wild once again. She sees would-be intruders lurking in the tangled vegetation on the slope below, ready to ascend the parapets. For a few minutes she feels herself as exposed and vulnerable as these Ming soldiers must have felt.

After a while, she turns towards the other end of the tower and gazes at the view further north through the open archway. The Great Wall rises and dips along the ridgeline of an endless mountain, sharp-edged against the blue sky and framed by the dark contours of the archway. It is studded at regular intervals by a succession of at least twenty watchtowers in one direction, and twenty more in the opposite. The morning sun, not yet at its zenith, lights up one face of the towers, adding drama to the darkness of the other sides still in shadow.

No camera could do justice to such a striking spectacle, but B has no other way to record, however inadequately, what she wants to share with her family. However transient each minute of this Chinese trip is, it will remain etched on her mind as a precious engraving, as should have been every minute of Eric's life. If only she had sensed it at the time. She waits until no other member of the group is obstructing the magnificent view. Unlike them, she prefers her pictures of the Great Wall without people. It should stand by itself, proclaim its majestic and inescapable presence, be left undisturbed by incongruous twenty-first-century sentinels.

Past this watchtower, a level stretch of walkway leads some fifty metres ahead to another hollow three-storey tower of similar shape and size, topped with a small turret surrounded by battlements. The group follow the corridor through this tower and find themselves outside, facing a further climb that takes them past a line of obstacle walls to a third watchtower situated in a dominating position. This impressive line of defence, seemingly untouched by the forces of nature to which it had been exposed for centuries, has been renovated.

Somehow the last few days have changed B. First, Alan was a remarkable and much needed interpreter of the Great Wall for her, but now she has less need of an intermediary. At this instant, she requires no explanation to appreciate the Great Wall as a formidable barrier. It is addressing her directly, openly revealing its secrets. She admires the genius of Qi Jiguang as a military strategist, able to realise in such a short time his grandiose vision of linking towers into a comprehensive system of defence. He knew how to combine the natural advantages of the terrain with the best tactics to raise the alarm effectively, to prevent surprise attacks, or to send troops along the fortified line if the enemy broke through. As a twenty-first-century trekker, B is able to cover the distance between these three towers rapidly. She can see for herself how essential it was for the sixteenth-century sentinels and soldiers to be able to do so to repel ferocious attackers.

The group stands now at the start of a continuous roller coaster of mountain ridges straddled by a very damaged Wall. What a stark contrast with the few hundred metres of reconstructed section on which they have just walked. Ahead of them, the seventh-century Jinshanling Wall has not been repaired since it was reinforced by the Ming General Qi Jiguang over four centuries ago. It is a ruin, but a splendid ruin, dotted at regular distances by extraordinary asperities. Upright sections of watchtowers jut out of heaps of rubble, as if pointing a defiant finger to the sky to proclaim that even if broken they have survived undefeated.

The next stretch is a perilous one-hundred-metre descent at a sixty-degree angle. The treads of this staircase are only half as deep as an average foot length and the steps are no more than crumbling and unstable stones. There is no other way to avoid tripping than to walk sideways, one foot at a time, and close to what remains of the parapet. B hears someone asking,

'How far did you say Simatai is, Alan?'

'Oh, ten kilometres, that's all.'

'Only ten kilometres? ... Ten kilometres of that?'

'Don't worry, only half of it is downhill, the other half is uphill and much safer to climb.'

While everyone is laughing at Alan's acquired British sense of irony, B is the only one feeling ecstatic at the prospect of being challenged at last and for a whole day. There is no rational explanation for the fact that, having to test her stamina, to rely on her sense of balance, to trust her ageing body, makes her feel alive and almost deliriously happy. Why this prospect fills her with gratitude tinged with sadness is a question she will ask herself and learn to answer satisfactorily, but only by the end of her Chinese pilgrimage.

Part of the next watchtower protrudes out of the Wall. It could have been a three-storey tower, who knows? All that remains is a large square platform of cracked stone slabs, supporting on three sides a few damaged brick pillars between dilapidated walls with arched openings. Nothing above it but the sky.

What are they hearing all of a sudden? Are these stones producing music? Inside the remains of the tower, the group

132

discovers a little old man perched on top of a heap of rubble in a corner. He is blowing into a long thin tube with a small upturned cup at the end. A piece of string hangs from the middle of that strange instrument with an intriguing collection of tiny colourful objects attached to its end. The man is motionless, keeping his eyes closed while blowing. B approaches to have a closer look at the dangling merchandise. Nothing could astonish and amuse her more than to find it composed of a few spherical red bells, a yellow rubber duck, and two small plastic Teletubbies - a purple Tinky Winky, and a green Dipsy -.

What a splendid opportunity for a picture. In the forefront, an old Chinese man in a crumpled outsize suit with two red paper flowers sticking out of his ancient skull cap, his shrivelled face facing the sun with closed eyes, his knobbly fingers holding an ingenious and pitiful display. All this for the sake of attracting, or maybe simply entertaining, a handful of possible customers. That touching silhouette, framed against the sky by the jagged openings in the wall of the dilapidated watchtower, with a background of ever-fading mountain ranges disappearing over the horizon, makes a stunningly dramatic tableau.

In a few weeks, she will show this picture to her husband and complement it with a mental image invested with meaning and emotions. Looking at it, she will hear the call of the 'over-the-horizon', silencing the sounds of the intruding consumer world and its futile knick-knacks. She will belong again to the mysterious triad of sky, earth and humanity. The line where the immense blue sky meets the vast expanse of earth, where the 'here' takes you to the 'beyond', will hold her in thrall. He will be happy for her that such a scene captured on film has reawakened in her the desire to keep walking towards the far away space that life holds open for you, even in your darkest hours. He will rejoice that her trek to recover some meaning in her life has been a successful rescue mission.

Alan indicates that it is time to leave behind the solitary hawker and move on. B is the first one to sling her small backpack over her shoulder and begins to climb up the steps leading to the next watchtower. For the next two hours on this Jinshanling Wall, she is no more than a pair of walking boots moving in cadence. She is not walking towards something, she is not walking away from anything, she is trusting the ancient colossus lying at her feet to take her where life wants her to be. The soothing silence of its stones covers any discordance in her mind, and keeps her in a peaceful place. Face to face with herself, she has escaped the flow of time.

Overwhelmed by a confused joy and aflame with energy, she scampers up and down crumbling stones, skipping along the walkway from one watchtower to another. All of them are slightly different and in various stages of deterioration. In a few of them, she is able to reach what remains of upper platforms that have lost their parapets, to stand at the edge, fearless of the plunging drop below her. For B, nothing can beat the exhilaration of standing on a few stone slabs, thirty metres above the slope, enjoying an eagle's view of a cascade of mountain crests and deep valleys.

The steeper the slopes, the higher the steps, the more excited she feels. She takes more and more risks. What is preventing her from falling? Alan wouldn't want to reprimand her. Perhaps he chooses to let Eric be the one protecting his mother from harm?

At the end of another steep climb, they find themselves overlooking a large artificial lake. An abrupt descent down deep steps takes them to a narrow bridge crossing over the end of that reservoir. This is no more than a few wooden planks forming a walkway suspended some fifty metres above the water by two long cables fixed to the rock. What a contrast between the ancient massive structure of stone, now so familiar, and this recently assembled framework. Such a fragile construction brings to mind the images of hazardous crossings above precipices on dangling lianas that one sees on television programmes.

The path on the other side widens to accommodate a small booth where Alan stops to explain the situation.

'You've walked the last ten kilometres of the Jinshanling Wall. Well done. As a treat, I give you the choice between walking to reach the Simatei guest house at the other end of this water, or using a zip wire.'

'A zip wire!' exclaims the chorus line of the startled group

'Anything's better than taking one more step,' says Jimmy always keen to sit down and enjoy a cool beer.

'Have you looked at that zip wire?' interrupts a horrified voice, stressing the 'that.' 'You'd be mad to trust your life to such a flimsy contraption.'

It has to be said that the starting point of the ride is indeed unpromising. There is a small platform and a ramshackle hut clinging to the edge of an abrupt fifty-metre drop. A noise indicates that a motor is running inside. A cable loop comes in and out of the hut wall through two holes, with a cut plastic bottle stuck in each of them, and stretches from one end of the lake to the other and back, over a distance of five hundred metres. Who would have thought of such a cheap arrangement rather than an industrial lubricant to ensure smooth running of the cable? As might be expected, it is that quirky detail that makes B instantly forget her understandable hesitation. Come what may, she has got to try it.

It is with something of a thrill that she steps onto the platform after having watched Jimmy and a few others leaving it to become small dots in the distance. Forgetting her initial apprehension, she introduces her legs into the two leather hoops dangling at the end of the thin pole attached to the moving cable, and lets the assistant tie her to it with a strap around her waist. One push, and she is off, hanging some forty metres above the water. With one hand shading her eyes, dazzled by the low sun, and the other tightly gripping the thin pole, she throws herself backwards. Her legs, now high above her head, dance a jig on the floor of the sky to the beat of her cries of delight. Weightless, young and carefree again, she is gliding in a limpid sky without racing dark clouds or furious winds to upset the ride, wishing it to last for ever.

Even if it is only later that these few moments of boundless excitement will assume their real significance in B's life, they are already the high point of the day. After her exhibition as a trapeze artist, the touchdown at the opposite end of the lake, a few metres from a small guest house, is close to a disappointment. Entering its walled courtyard and dragging her suitcase to another small en suite bedroom with brownish water in the pipes, now feels like a banal routine.

Later, at the dinner table, she is newly willing to add her voice to the general conversation while sharing the tasty home-made dishes served by smiling young girls in uniform. She is eager to compare notes with the rest of the company, before retiring to her room to slide inside her silk liner. The long hours of physical exertion in the open air require her mind to fall instantly into deep sleep and prevent her from re-living her prowess in her dreams.

9½   Reflections

What's happening to me, GM? Why is it that today I don't come to you full of anger against myself, and against the world? Lucky you, to be spared my dreary waffle for once! Yes, I'll say it, today was a beautiful day. I enjoyed it without remorse. Can you believe that?

Trekking for hours in a magnificent expanse of earth and sky, I felt more resolute than I thought I would ever be again. Above all, I'll never forget how happy I was communing with my Great Wall. A rock-solid friend, in every sense of the word. That's what it is for me. I see its dauntless presence under my feet and all the way to the edge of the sky. I trust and enjoy its twists and turns. We share secrets. It's telling me about its haunting past and I'm eager to relive it in its company. Isn't it funny how it helps me to make sense of what will always threaten to toss me into dark waves? Yes, it teaches me tricks to climb out of the unavoidable Eric-shaped holes on my path. It even encourages me to accept the role of survivor, without feeling too guilty.

I've been aware and convinced for many years now that being absorbed in the sad events of one's past should not be discouraged, as so often happens. It's a natural need. It does not, absolutely not, amount to a blameworthy or unhealthy refusal to live in the present. Under no circumstances would I use the awful cliché, 'Life must go on.' Nor do I ever intend to do so, particularly with bereaved parents. It is meaningless and, above all, cruel. What life will go on for Eric? It's only the amended cliché, 'Life without Eric must go on,' that I can ever use. Sorry, but my past is for ever my present and my future. There is no page to turn.

During the few minutes when I hung from a zip wire this afternoon, I was not far from attaining the early stage of Zen, and experiencing the Satori feeling of infinite space and time. It was as if I had jettisoned ballast, and was free to soar into the sky. But let's come back to earth. It's while walking on that Great Wall that I'm able to frame and blur together in my mind past, present and future. It's only then that I can truly escape the tyranny of human time. I feel able to jump over its hurdles of 'never again', of 'too late', of 'if only'.

Ahead of me, and behind me, I see the sky clinging to the Great Wall as it crests the mountains. And, day after day, and just because it's there, I have to walk the distance between myself and the horizon. It acts on me both as a mysterious invitation to keep on climbing, just for the sake of climbing, and as the promise of approaching answers that I have been seeking for all these years. Will that promise be fulfilled? At times I am tempted to say, 'Yes, I believe so.' But the question of when still agitates me.

And you, GM, what do you think? Walking on that path with you and your silences, is it part of the game of life you play with all of us? No doubt, you make the rules and, to play it, we have to accept them. But rules have to make sense to the players, don't they? Do you think they make sense to me? Do you hope they will one day? You could at least answer that last question. It would comfort me.

You're faithful and I like having you with me. But who wants a silent companion? Not me, and you know me well enough to realise that. I need answers. I won't stop arguing with you until I hear your voice. I might turn down the volume of my inner monologues, but don't expect more than that. Enough of playing the enigmatic with me!

10

The Mutianyu Great Wall

A knock at the door startles B out of deep sleep. Still dreaming in the first few seconds preceding her return to the real world, she hears herself saying, '*J'ai trop pleuré! Les aubes sont nâvrantes,*' and adding immediately, 'but this has nothing to do with me.' Fully awake now, she reflects on that short dream. Why did she say, '*I have wept too much! The dawns are heartbreaking*'? Why indeed should the new dawn bring her distress? Of course it happened to her regularly in the past, but since she has left home, she feels able to distance herself from that past with all the painful years of growing older without Eric. Here in China, her mornings are no longer full of despair. They are full of promise, and she welcomes each one of them. It does not surprise her that, even in her semi-conscious state, she rejects that line of Rimbaud as totally inappropriate. No need for poetical gloom.

She is happy to greet the day, but only slowly aware that it is Emma knocking at the door. 'Early start today, remember! Our coach is leaving soon.' Of course, she would rather wake up at the crack of dawn, as she did in the first days of the trek. Being later than usual, she has to face the problem of finding some privacy in this shared bedroom while getting ready in a hurry. Her room-mate is quite relaxed about it, but agrees amiably that they should take turns in the lockless bathroom and always knock whether entering or leaving it. Soon, they are both frantically packing and pushing their luggage outside the door to be collected by the coach driver. More members of the group come out of the few rooms looking out onto the square courtyard. This is a small guest house and it cannot accommodate larger parties than the NewShores volunteers, but its restaurant is spacious enough to be open to the locals also. For the first time in the trip, Chinese voices dominate their breakfast.

Simatai is the end of the line for first-time trekkers on the Great Wall. They have to alight and come down to the valley. The stone colossus rides on eastwards all the way to the Bohai Bay, the innermost gulf of the Yellow Sea. But today, after centuries of neglect, that section does not tolerate the presence of foolhardy intruders. It is extremely hazardous, impassable even. To achieve the goal of their fundraising challenge of walking 100 kilometres, the group has to turn around and drive back towards Beijing where stretches of the Great Wall closer to the city have been extensively restored.

There is not much to see during the two-hour trip on the brand new multi-lane expressway that never deviates from the straight line pointing directly towards the capital. The skinny silhouettes of young leafless trees lining the road cannot hide the vast and empty expanses of flat stony ground, the colour of dust, on each side. What a contrast with the craggy high ground of the YanShan Mountains. B gives a sigh. No twinge of excitement. Why does she feel lonely and despondent sitting in this comfortable coach? Is it too far-fetched to believe that she is missing her daily dose of Great Wall?

Watching the strategies of the drivers in the various vehicles that occupy the wrong lanes captivates her attention for a while. Rusty old trucks and overloaded three-wheelers will not budge from the fast lane once they have found a way to enter it.

Private cars and regular taxis with B-licence plates whizz past looking for a gap and honking in the hope of creating one. Only the cyclists ride obediently on the right-hand side.

When the coach leaves the motorway and comes to a halt in the outskirts of Beijing, the sun, at its zenith, lights up the scene. It gives a healthy glow to the dull low houses and anonymous shops of this sprawling suburb. The people on the street smile at each other. B steps out, her camera at the ready, having noticed a small toddler confidently holding a young woman's hand. She stoops to strike up a conversation with him, or at least to convey her interest in the toy in his other hand, and to encourage him to show it to her. At the same time, her camera clicks in the face of the shy little boy. The corners of his tiny mouth sink downwards towards his chin as he tries desperately not to cry. To avoid a diplomatic incident, she stands up swiftly and starts an apologetic pantomime supposed to demonstrate her pure intentions, and to express her admiration to the young mother. Any kind of praise of a child or of a pet is instantly understood and always accepted joyfully by its owner.

The exchange between B and the young Chinese woman, each conducting a one-sided conversation in their own tongue, could not be more friendly if they had known each other for years. Reassured at last, the little boy decides to hold out his hand and share his treasure. This is the right time to take a picture of mother and child smiling at the camera. In the meantime, after a short pause in a small roadside café, the group comes out and B joins them on the coach while addressing a few more excited 'Bye-byes' to the young family.

An hour later, they arrive at the village of Mutianyu and stop at the edge of it, on the side of a small roundabout. 'That's it,' announces Alan, 'we walk from here to reach the Great Wall.'

After sitting in the air-conditioned coach all morning, everybody welcomes Emma's inescapable routine outside in the cool breeze. She chooses a small area safe from the cars circling around the grassy centre of the roundabout, where a young woman is grazing a horse. While they are obeying the tour leader's instructions, bending and stretching arms and legs, a car stops abruptly next to them. A giggling couple jump out of it, holding cameras, and begin snapping the scene. General laughter ensues. Life outside her native country has taught B to enjoy, rather than criticize, differences and similarities in the ways we see each other. The present incident reminds her of a poem by the German poet Stefan George about a panther in a cage giving his thoughts on the zoo visitors looking at him.

To end the warm-up session with a few minutes of doubling-up and shaking with laughter is a deep-breathing exercise for the soul. It puts the group in a joyful mood to begin the walk onto a country road off the roundabout. After a couple of hours hiking at the bottom of low foothills, they pass clusters of small farmhouses that could be abandoned, if it were not for a few rustic farming tools and baskets lying around. That agglomeration is in fact a hamlet called Beigo, not even worth a mention in the description of today's programme printed in the tour brochure that B checks each morning. But, as we shall see, it merits a mention in this story.

On entering that small village, B realises that she has made a big mistake. She should have seized the opportunity for a 'comfort stop' at the small café, as everybody else did, instead of taking pictures and chatting with the locals. Soon, her situation will turn into an emergency. What can she do? Fortunately Jimmy, the tour doctor, happens to be walking next to her. He will not be shocked by her allusion to a bodily function. They have just reached the section of the road that appears to be the main and only street of Beigo. And, Oh miracle, together they spot on the sidewalk a small windowless brick cube. A Chinese sign points to an opening on the side that must be the entrance, though it lacks a proper door. Trusting her nose, B can decide without any doubt that this purpose-built construction is the communal lavatory freely available to the inhabitants of most Chinese villages to help them save water. She enters it cautiously, and when her eyes get used to the dark, she spots along the back wall a tiny elderly woman crouching above one of the six circular holes cut in the concrete floor. 'Oh! I am terribly sorry!' she exclaims, rushing outside. This first attempt at finding a solution to her personal problem has failed miserably. She must improve her strategy.

As soon as the Chinese woman has left, she asks Jimmy to stand in front of the entrance with the impossible mission of barring access in any language he can muster and, if needed, with forbidding gestures, to anyone else while she is inside. Needless to say that she comes out in record time, having felt a mixture of fear and disgust. Perversely, she is also grateful for this embarrassing but uniquely exciting experience. What a wonderful anecdote to recount at dinner parties. Will she evoke the rank stench that no sweet-smelling perfumes could eradicate? Will she describe the shock of catching a glimpse directly through that round hole of sewage flowing freely along at no more than a metre below her? Let us drop the subject for the moment.

Soon, B and Jimmy catch up with the rest of the group as they turn onto a narrow country lane. Further on, it leads up a steep hillside covered with gorse, dried-up bushes and stunted trees. Scrambling up the path of dry earth to reach the Great

Wall is going to be arduous and uncomfortable. By now, the air is unusually warm and humid.

Alan begins the ascent leading the way at a remarkably fast pace, and is soon hidden from view by the tangled vegetation covering the hillside. Undaunted, everyone in the group is eager to follow him. They intend to meet the present challenge bravely, exchanging jokes and laughing while rushing upwards. No doubt, they will have to pause or even collapse out of breath many times along the slope, before accepting that mountaineering requires one not to laugh in the face of adversity. B's way to prove to herself that she is up to the task of tackling any increased incline is altogether more controlled. Years of walking holidays with her husband have taught her that you ignore your body's limitations at your peril. She sets a slow pace from the start, begins to use each step to impose a regular rhythm on her breathing, and walks on determinedly silent. Giggling or talking is out of the question. She wants to carry on steadily all the way to the top without slumping onto the ground totally exhausted and gasping for air.

The slope is getting steeper and soon she finds herself alone, way ahead of the others. Bent close to the ground, she is almost crawling along the narrow slippery path, holding on to low branches when possible. It is, in a certain measure, a comfort not to see how far ahead the ridge of the hill is. After what seems like an eternity, the Great Wall looms above her. What a relief to come face to face with that old and faithful friend awaiting her, as promised, at the crest of the mountain. She ducks and heaves herself through the narrow archway cut in its parapet. Alan grabs her hand to pull her onto a small platform on the walkway. Today, given her level of fatigue, she does not see it as a loss of dignity to accept, and even welcome, his help.

Right now, she can do no more than remain sprawled on the cool stone slabs, beads of perspiration dripping from her face and along her neck, and getting her breath back.

As soon as she begins to feel her normal self again, she decides that the only way to recuperate fully is to eat the picnic provided this morning by the guest house, without waiting for the others. When she cracks open her hard-boiled egg it reveals a reddish yoke in the first stage of becoming a chick. She sends it flying over the parapet. Fortunately, the banana and the large piece of cake look safe enough and indeed they taste delicious. Nothing could be more refreshing to help her flush them down her parched throat than the contents of her two bottles of water. Today, for the first time, dehydration is a real threat.

When at last one member of the group appears at the parapet's archway, he is in his turn greeted and hoisted up by Alan, before collapsing on the ground breathing with difficulty, just like B earlier. By now she has fully recovered and looks eager to move on. How selfish of her, she thinks briefly, but her leg muscles will not remain inactive much longer without stiffening and refusing to be serviceable for the rest of the afternoon. That is a real risk at her age, especially after the tremendous efforts they had to make earlier. How can she avoid it, she wonders.

Unable to control her rising impatience any longer, she turns to Alan pointing above her at an offshoot of the Great Wall leading to a ruined watchtower. 'I am sure it will be some time before everybody is here. While they rest and eat their picnic, would it be possible to dash up there to see the view and come back quickly. Is that all right?' Her request does not seem to astonish Alan who nods with an amused smile, 'Oh, that's no problem, B. You're a good walker. Off you go.'

She would not have run faster to the steps leading up to the tower if she had been trying to escape a swarm of bees. If there are very few bees, if any, there are quite a few walkers. To her surprise, she finds herself almost having to fight her way through a mix of Chinese families and western tourists.

After spending the first few days in blissful isolation on the Great Wall, immersing herself in its meaningful magnificence, communicating with its silent past, she resents the crowd. A familiar feeling of loss, of 'no-more', invades her. She has naïvely taken for granted what is only a short-lived privilege. She must resign herself to accepting the presence of more trekkers, not seeing them as usurpers of her special treat. Vigorous exercise will help her to refuel her mind with dopamine before its level and her mood drop. It never fails with her. And what better opportunity than ascending the few hundred metres leading to the watchtower above her.

Progressively, the paved incline gets steeper and small steps are built into the slope roughly a metre apart. Soon the number of steps increases and the space between them becomes shorter. If it gets harder to climb them, that is nothing compared with the next section. What is usually a sloping ramp to access a watchtower, is here a long and almost vertical flight of steps, less than a metre wide, between the two parapets. To add an extra frisson to the climb, the tread of this seemingly unending stairway is only half as deep as the length of an average foot. Handrails run on each side of that narrow stone ladder cut roughly in the rock, and B grabs them as a lifebelt. Having counted already fifty steps, and being only halfway up that devilish passage, she realises how presumptuous and foolish she was to think she could make such an effort. It is impossible to back down now, as a couple of young non-Chinese trekkers are right behind her, and squeezing past them would risk their lives and hers. She must soldier on, and soldier on she will.

Until this moment she has never had a chance to test to its limit the strength of her instinct for survival. Until now she has never been so confident that someone is watching over her and protecting her wherever she is. She can also count on her new friend, the Great Wall, to make sure she comes to no harm while he carries her towards her goal.

No words could describe adequately her desperate efforts to scramble up those last steps. Suffice it to say that she reaches the end of that vertiginous ladder crawling on her stomach and being unceremoniously hoisted onto the small platform of the ruined watchtower by sympathetic hands that prop her against what remains of a partly destroyed side wall. At the opposite end, an archway is still standing, but cracked bricks piled up across it block the access. Beyond it the Great Wall is no more than a track made of loose broken steps and crumbling stones still clinging to the hill crest. It is clearly impassable.

The youngsters who have arrived on the watchtower platform with B are not casting kindly eyes on her. Far from it. Having to wait behind an older person is unbearable. And now that they have no way to escape, she makes them listen to her telling them, 'I'm 68, you know. Wait until you're my age and you'll see how slow you'll be!' Instead of a gratifying reply, all she gets is a look that says eloquently, 'Why can't you keep quiet, woman, and get lost?' Oh well, after all, she should not have gone on the offensive like that, but we ought to forgive her; she is worn out and can hardly think straight at the moment.

The only reward she wants is that nothing and no one should prevent her from enjoying the glorious spectacle awaiting intrepid and courageous climbers who have reached this elevated viewpoint. The purpose of a watchtower like this one is to command a strategic position and to allow the Ming soldiers to keep watch from a superior height. Instead of aesthetic pleasure, they must have experienced a combination of terror and intense boredom. But today it offers B the chance to admire those endless chains of mountains rippling away eastward and westward, with the snaking Mutianyu Great Wall pinned to their ridges by numerous watchtowers. For the sake of it, she waves at her group sitting in the shade of a parapet far below her listening to Alan's description of the rest of the day. But no one is looking at her.

Returning is not the gruelling experience of the way up. Nevertheless, having to negotiate the shallow steps of the stone ladder backwards is quite frightening. In comparison, the last two-thirds of the descent are easy. There are fewer tourists and B cannot resist the temptation to hurtle down the slope, hopping from one step to the next. What was bound to happen, happens. Landing at speed, with one of her boots caught at the heel by the edge of a step, and the tip of it tilting over and scraping the ground, she stumbles. She would have tumbled over if an elderly Chinese man with lightning reflexes had not grasped her sleeve to stop her fall. With her eyes constantly lowered to check where she is putting her feet, and her heart still thumping in her chest, she rejoins the group. Everyone is getting ready for the sixth Great Wall walk of the challenge. They are heading eastward. She follows them sheepishly, without a last look behind her at the watchtower that could have sent her to hospital.

From the start, the Mutianyu Great Wall imposes its massive presence on her. But, stretching in front of her, as impressive and grandiose as it still is, it is also different. The whole structure looks sturdy, a perfectly renovated Ming Wall. No more crumbling steps, nor shorn-off side walls, no watchtowers in ruins. The walkway built with stone slabs is never less than six or seven metres wide. With its rampart as high in places as twenty metres above the slope, it is like a long elevated corridor between grey-bricked crenellated parapets. Somehow, the wild beast seems to have been tamed and prepared for show. And instead of riding bare rocky crags and ridges, it is now roaming over more hospitable territory, following a softer line of lofty mountains and foothills densely covered with dark green forests.

The tower-to-tower walk is often level between long stretches of up-and-down inclines that are steep, but never as demanding as those of the Jinshanling Great Wall or the Simatai Great Wall. Even the blue of the sky is different here, a shade duller because of a thin haze.

Something is missing from that scenery. In B's mind the flow of tourists around her metamorphose into Ming soldiers moving from one watchtower to another, ready to repel a nomad attack. Conjuring up that army with their shouted orders resonating in her ears, joining them to march purposefully on, is her way of escaping disappointment. She needs a feeling of participation to extend the precious time of communion with the Great Wall. Re-living its past history has a bracing effect on her; something new and intense arises within her.

As if he wanted to interrupt her musing, Alan stops on the ramp leading to the next watchtower. He signals a short pause to rest and drink, but looks eager to provide the group with some information. Before he has time to open his mouth after drinking from his water bottle, B cannot refrain from speaking.

'Alan, why is it that the parapets are crenellated on both sides?' Does she not see that her enthusiastic questioning might appear as showing off?

'Let me come to that, B, in good time. A little bit of history first. Remember that the risk of invasion from the north by the nomadic tribes of the steppes was always there. In the sixth century, the Northern Qi dynasty built walls of rammed earth and stones to protect the northern frontiers. It didn't always help. In the thirteenth century, the Mongols, ruled by Kublai Khan, Genghis Khan's grandson, invaded and conquered China and founded the Mongol-led Yuan Dynasty. They governed the Empire from 1271 till 1368 when the ethnic Han Chinese rebelled successfully and established the Ming dynasty that lasted for almost three centuries.

'Beijing became the imperial city and in 1406 the construction of the imperial palace, the Forbidden City, began, ending in 1420. By that time, it was essential to have a stronger system of defence against northern invaders and the Wall was reinforced. But in 1449, a Mongol army of 50,000 surrounded and massacred a Chinese army of half a million at the battle of Tumu. The Emperor was captured. Periodic raiding continued and the Mongol leader, Altan Khan, reached the outskirts of Beijing, just inside the Great Wall. Qi Jiguang - you remember that famous general - helped to defeat him. In 1568, at the age of forty, he was called upon to train the troops and to upgrade the Great Wall.

'We owe to him the Ming Great Wall that you see today between Beijing and the Yellow Sea. He faced the parapets with identical bricks, made wide walkways with stone slabs. He added watchtowers that allowed troops and arms to be sheltered or rushed easily along the top to where the enemy threatened to attack. By the way, local granite was used here and made the Wall more durable, but it was also renovated in 1984 when the government decided to make it safe for tourists.

'So, you see, B, here, only 70 kilometres away from Beijing, the nomads had threatened and been able to break the line of defence many times. The Chinese needed crenellated battlements on the outside and the inside of the Wall to be able to shoot at them coming from either direction.'

As soon as Alan ends his long and well-rehearsed presentation, loud applause erupts, coming not so much from the Newshores group as from a wide audience of tourists who have stopped to listen to him. A painful cramp in her right hand, resulting from scribbling frantically in her notebook, prevents B from using it efficiently, but not from exclaiming loudly, 'Bravo and thank you, Alan, you're brilliant!'

For the next hour, it is possible to stride along level stretches, or to manage the slopes without having to slow down to a crawl. Here on the Mutianyu Great Wall every step and the Wall floor have been superbly repaired, and are actually safer than many pavements at home. Following Epictetus' advice, 'Man, if you are anybody, go walking alone, converse with yourself,' B is following the group, wrapped in her own thoughts. Gradually, she becomes aware of a thin musical tune that sounds Chinese but is also familiar. As she walks on and comes closer to its source, she could swear she has heard that music before. But where? Suddenly she recognises it. It can't be! It is Vivaldi's piccolo concerto. She had heard it a couple of years before on the radio, and had bought the CD to dance to its joyful and bouncing rhythm with her youngest granddaughter. Italian baroque music used as musak on the Great Wall of China! What next?

Having arrived at the next hilltop after climbing an unusually long and steep flight of steps, she discovers on the other side what can only be described as a Chinese version of Disneyland. Red cable car cabins shuttling tourists between the Wall and the valley below, compete with a chairlift on a parallel route two hundred metres apart. Now she sees why her group have been the only ones scrambling up the steep slope this morning.

People queue at a small stall to buy tickets. B forgets her disappointment when Alan explains that here the slippery downhill path is so treacherous that it is better to use mechanised transport. The choice is between hanging from a wire high in the air or squeezing her body into a tiny wheeled toboggan for a ride down a huge helter-skelter winding all the way to the bottom of the valley. Taking a glance at it, she understands why continuous background music does not cover the screams of fear and excitement rising from the slope below the Wall. Well, on reflection, why not follow the when-in-Rome-do-as-the-Romans-do principle in China as well? She will join the few intrepid members of the group who are not tempted by the cable car or chair lift.

As soon as she is sitting safely in her tight-fitting vehicle, the attendant points at a tall panel with explanatory drawings and instructions in English. She is third in the queue, and soon he sends her on her way downhill. Pushing away from her a long-handled brake attached to the floor between her legs comes naturally and slows down the toboggan. But despite her efforts to sit further away, to be able to pull the handle towards her and go faster instead, gravity throws her forward. She would love to experience the thrill of speed, but has to settle for the fear of being ejected at each sharp turn.

At the bottom, after extracting herself from her toboggan when it comes to a stop, she finds herself confronted by two fake Ming soldiers in armour. One of them threatens to chop her head off with a long sabre-like sword, while the other points to a sign offering to take her picture for a few yuans. Such a travesty of history would have been the last straw for B, if she had not wisely capitulated and accepted at last to leave her carapace of intellectual snobbery and join the game. She has got to show her granddaughters the picture of a terrified grandmother with a sharp sword against her neck, ready to be slaughtered by two ferocious warriors.

Further along the road, the group discovers a row of colourful clothes stalls with a few bigger shops behind them, spilling their wares onto the pavement. They are besieged by hordes of tourists originating from every continent. Above one stall, a huge board says under its Chinese and inevitable Coca Cola signs, 'State-TVN Tourist Devdlopment All-Aroun Dstore'. State intervention is a fact of life in China. But whatever their political tendencies and desires not to collude with any authoritarian regime, nobody in the British group can resist the attraction of silky clothes floating in the breeze.

B is soon pursued by a charming Chinese girl trying to persuade her to buy a silk bathrobe. Hoping to discourage her unwelcome attentions by saying, 'Not now, later,' is of course the worst mistake. After rummaging frantically through piles of silk displayed on tables, or hanging from wires stretched across the canvas roof of the stalls, she finds at last four blue silk pyjamas in the correct sizes for her granddaughters. When she hesitates to purchase them, the seller actually offers to lower the price. Once in the grip of bargaining fever, it is impossible to leave empty-handed. For B, the prospect of seeing her girls in these lovely outfits fills her with a joy that submerges her humanitarian concerns.

Having allowed enough time for a profitable shopping spree, as Alan was certainly expected to do as a state-accredited tour guide, he takes the group down the road that leads to the small continental-style hotel. B is in two minds about this seventh night. No more Chinese *je-ne-sais-quoi* now that they have arrived in the village of Mutianyu, but the prospect of taking a shower and sleeping between cotton sheets in a proper bed tilts the scales. Why not see the bright side and skip regrets? She knows that her friend the Great Wall is neither cheap nor tame.

As is often the case with B, at the point of falling asleep, she yearns to go back to the safety of her mother tongue. Her last thought is of '*la Grande Muraille de Chine.*' Each word in French has a voice that speaks to her. Together they sing a paean to invincibility. They resonate in her head, and trail away lulling her to sleep.

Let her enjoy a peaceful night with pleasant dreams, or perhaps no dreams at all.

10½   Reflections

Another wonderful day with the Great Wall, GM. Each time it sends good vibes to me. How can I explain it better than by saying that the bond with it gives me a real sense of direction, opens a door to a world where I walk with Eric at my side, no more a world without him. A new resolve to journey forward in that world is growing inside me.

This trek has brought joy and the promise of more joys ahead, and has given me the strength to face the pain that is part of my life and will always be. Riding the crests of the beautiful YanShan mountains, hiking along the Great Wall, never retracing my steps, always forwards, that's the way to go in my life.

I've railed against you, GM, implored you to answer my questions, but I've got to confess that I'm also grateful to you. Despite your silence, you've ways to make me feel good, to help me to see more clearly inside myself.

And don't ask me why, GM, but I am confident that you'll keep me safe and in good health during this trip. Do you remember only a month ago how I could hardly put my swollen foot on the ground? Now, I am sure that I won't need antibiotics here. Why do you raise your eyebrows, GM? Is that your way of asking why I carry a box of them in my luggage? Oh, come on, GM, be more tolerant. I'm only human, I need talismans, just to be sure. Do I detect a half-smile crossing your face? I'm so glad you have a sense of humour!

Of course, counting on you to keep me safe doesn't allow me to behave foolishly as if I were indestructible. I blame myself for taking silly risks on this walk. When I reached my limits on the vertical flight of steps this morning, for a few seconds I thought the worst was going to happen to me, but my instinct for survival saved me. I had not felt it since Eric died. Did you contrive this dangerous situation, just to convince me that it is still intact and strong? Well, GM, you've succeeded.

And was there anything more stupid than running on the way down? Why can't I act my age? How right you were, GM, to make me stumble. I need such warnings to bring me to my senses. Thank you for sending that old Chinese man to save me in the nick of time from a nasty fall. In your place, I would have been tempted to abandon me to my fate. That's what I deserved.

Anyway, GM, today's trekking started gloriously and safely thanks to you and Eric. But I was disappointed that the second part led us to some kind of Disneyland. What have they done there to my Great Wall? Do they want to prevent me from admiring it, from being in awe of its grandeur? How could they violate its right to remain wild and free, to look splendid and fearless? They should celebrate its powerful presence, not abuse it for trivial purposes. I found the end of today's hike a real let-down. So, why did I resign myself to enjoying the cheap thrills on offer to tourists? What else could I do? But, in a sense, GM, it gave me the opportunity to see how my wonderful Wall bears it all with dignity. Whatever bizarre embellishments the Chinese can think of, they'll never be able to reduce its power to impress, nothing can tarnish its image. Its indomitable spirit can't be crushed. It knows no law but its own. Even under the trappings of vulgar entertainment, it still radiates conquering force.

I feel moved and uplifted by the positive message I receive from this magnificent structure, as much today as when I saw it for the first time. It urges me to believe in my own strength and resilience. It encourages me to

156

find my own way forward, with Eric as my guiding light. It tells me never to let that light fade. And it wants me to resist the pressure to conform to other people's expectations of me when they don't feel right for me.

Events since I signed up for this charity walk, convince me more than ever of Eric's presence in my life. They happen as gifts that I receive from him, always unexpectedly, and I like to think of myself as the lucky owner of a treasure chest in which I store them. The unshakeable belief that they make my life richer, and that more of them will come, fills me with joy.

Did you and Eric plan all that, GM? I suspect that both of you knew all along what would happen to me when you dropped that NewShores leaflet on my desk. I'm beginning to see through you, GM. But more about that tomorrow.

11

The Badaling Great Wall

This morning the sun is in hiding, a diffuse light in a hazy sky hardly penetrates the closed curtains of the bedroom. Had it not been for her alarm clock, B would have slept longer in that Mutianyu hotel bed. Now that she is awake, she certainly does not want to celebrate the improvement in her living conditions with a snooze. It would feel wrong to do so. The only improvement she welcomes with a clear conscience is the lock on her bathroom door. For her, privacy is a question of decency, not of luxury.

Glancing outside the window onto the empty hotel car park, she sees the tour driver already in the coach, reading a newspaper. Alan and Emma, wrapped tightly in their anoraks, greet members of the group rushing from the hotel to the restaurant. When she joins them outside, the unusually damp and grey haze is something of a shock. She does not mind the cold breeze, but where is the sun shining in a limpid sky that she has got used to? Dull and drizzly weather is totally unacceptable for her last walking day on the Great Wall. Nothing can weaken her conviction that the weather has no choice but to be on her side.

After the usual breakfast everyone gathers at the door of the coach, obviously eager to leave Mutianyu, or at least to escape the humid atmosphere and the threat of rain. What B wants above all is to take full advantage of that last day. To finish on a high note. She has checked its programme in the tour brochure this morning, and she is a little worried. It warns of the contrast between the remote tranquillity of the past few days and the bustling noisy crowds on the Badaling Great Wall, their final port of call.

B can observe through the windows of the coach taking the group to their next destination that there is already a change in the scenery. The three-lane expressway, bordered with small trees in bloom, soon becomes a two-lane road that looks more like a wide avenue with low two-storey flat-roofed buildings on either side. Road intersections with pedestrian crossings controlled by traffic lights announce that they are now in the outskirts of Beijing. In an effort to improve security, and to impose some discipline on the dangerous drivers and the careless pedestrians, big digits on the green lights indicate the countdown from sixty seconds until they change to red. B is on the edge of her seat, afraid to witness a fatal accident whenever they pass a slow overloaded three-wheeled motorcycle at full speed.

Her attention is soon caught by small groups of elderly workers, male and female, whose day job is to prettify the edges of the road. Some are repairing low walls along the sides; others are planting young trees, or watering flowering bushes growing in long concrete troughs. What could be, she wonders, the purpose of the old woman who is shovelling sand with a big spade from one heap to another next to it? Even Alan can do no better than to answer her with a smile.

To bypass Beijing, and to avoid the chaos created by speeding coaches, cars, bicycles, pedestrians, or being caught in traffic at a standstill, the coach driver turns onto a new toll motorway. After less than half an hour on the empty fast lane, he takes an exit with a sign showing for the first time the word 'Badaling' below the Chinese characters. The road is heading north through another suburb that makes no attempt to look attractive.

After a few hundred metres, the coach passes a long two-storey warehouse with a façade of opaque windows and a door at each end. Shining brightly against the dull sky, golden dragons and Chinese characters raised on thin metal rods run along the edge of the roof. Another sign underneath says in big letters, 'Friendship Store'. The coach turns into a vast parking area at the rear of the building and stops in front of one of two doors with a big sign, 'The Cloisonne Factory'. Alan jumps to his feet, seizing the microphone before anyone alights.

'We're going to stop here,' he announces, 'I'll take you to visit the factory first. You'll be able to watch the various stages of the metalworking technique called 'cloisonné'. It was invented in the Byzantine Empire but it reached China by the Silk Road seven hundred years ago in the Yuan Dynasty. Then we'll go to the store where you can buy objects they have made and other souvenirs. But you don't bargain here, the prices are fixed by the government.'

'Alan, there are two entrances, is there another store? What do they sell there?' asks someone, excited at the prospect of a shopping spree.

'It's the entrance for Chinese people, not for the tourists. But you would see exactly the same things there, anyway.'

'This is segregation, Alan. Why?'

'Oh, no, it's not segregation,' exclaims Alan, 'it's because the Chinese make a dreadful noise when they go shopping, and it disturbs tourists not used to it. In fact, they were originally set up to sell only to foreign tourists.'

It will be months later, when discussing her trip with friends that they question Alan's explanation. Could it be that the prices of what was sold to naïve tourists had been inflated, and that it was best to keep them unaware of it? But why spoil her memories of an enjoyable experience with futile doubts?

Inside the factory, young women in a row of small workshops are making cloisonné. A panel on the wall describes the various stages in that long process. Some of the workers are busy drawing intricate designs on pieces of copper of all shapes and sizes. Others are twisting, pasting and soldering copper filigree, painstakingly following the outlines of the drawings. Further on, others, surrounded by small cups of coloured enamel paste, use small pipettes to drop carefully tiny amounts of colour into each outlined section. Each piece is then subjected to intense heat. After the enamel firing process, it is polished and gilded.

The women working in the factory never take their eyes off their delicate tasks to look at the visitors watching them. Other women are sitting at tables around the walls in the vast shopping area that looks more like a warehouse, happy to demonstrate their various crafts. They are painting exquisite scenes on the insides of tiny bottles, reproducing pictures on large scrolls, carving lacquerware, enamelling porcelain vases, covering sheets of rice paper with calligraphy, or cutting complicated patterns in thin cardboard to create three-dimensional landscapes. Their skills are astonishing.

But the open-plan floor of that enormous store is mostly packed with tables overloaded with finished objects. Thousands of brightly-coloured articles in cloisonné and various decorative ornaments make it look like Aladdin's cave. As soon as they are let loose, the members of the group race off in all directions. Is it the sheer pleasure of following one's instinct rather than a guide, or is it simply shopping frenzy that overcomes them? From now on, it's every man for himself in that frantic search for the perfect gift, or the ideal souvenir.

After giving his charges free rein for almost an hour, Alan attempts to round them up. An impossible task. Some escape to rush just once more to the cashier's desk to buy another item. B is still rummaging among the displays, agonizing over adding another cloisonné panda or an enamelled mirror to her bulging shopping basket. At last he succeeds in corralling everyone and enticing, or in the end urging them, to board the coach. For the half-hour drive, he abandons the idea of giving information about the next walk. Even with his microphone, he cannot compete with the noise generated by deliriously happy customers comparing and discussing their purchases.

After a short tunnel cut through the mountain, they emerge into a narrow pass between densely-forested mountains. Soon the coach stops at the end of a long line of coaches parked on a vast area at the side of the road. The Great Wall is right there, extending across the valley and rising steeply to the mountain crests on either side. With lightning speed, B grabs the microphone before Alan can pick it up.

'I thought I ought to mention quickly that, even if the technique of cloisonné is Chinese, the word for it is not,' she announces in a professorial tone, 'it comes from the French word '*cloison*', meaning the space marked on the copper objects by the copper filigree, and later filled with coloured enamel."

No doubt, if the group could vote out one of its members, B would have been expelled long ago. But she is lucky that Alan, as always the perfect diplomat, decides wisely to take his turn at the microphone to cover the whispered, 'There she goes again!' and 'Why can't she keep quiet?'

'Listen, you guys,' he interrupts, 'we've arrived at Badaling. in the Jundu mountains, sixty kilometres north of Beijing. We're in the defile that Kublai Khan, Genghis Khan's grandson, took

162

to invade the capital. OK, let me refresh your memory quickly. As you know, Kublai Khan conquered the whole of China and founded the first Mongol dynasty, the Yuan dynasty in 1271. It lasted until 1368, when they were overthrown, and Chinese rule was restored by the Ming dynasty.

'Its first Emperor, Zhu Yuanzhang, wanted to extend and strengthen the old Qin network of long walls to block the regular incursions by the nomads, mostly through the mountain passes around Beijing, at Badaling and at Gubeikou. In Ming times, it wasn't called 'Chang Cheng', the term used was 'Chiu-Pien-Chen', the Nine Borders Garrisons. As you know, it was Qi Jiguang's idea to create a defensive system of garrisons and watchtowers. That way, soldiers could be deployed quickly along the frontier to wherever needed.

'You've walked on other parts of the Ming Wall, but here at Badaling you have a chance to see and admire the strategic significance of the Great Wall. It makes this pass and this steep mountainous terrain almost impregnable. Deng Xiaoping launched a programme of restoration in 1984 with his slogan, 'Love China and Rebuild the Great Wall', and you see it here restored to how it was six hundred years ago, when the Ming reinforced the old structure with bricks and stones. Every visiting foreign head of state is taken to Badaling. It attracts millions of visitors and never fails to impress them.'

'It certainly doesn't impress me,' mutters B to herself. How can she not feel disappointed as she looks at this artificial reincarnation, with everything so pristine? Brand new like that, the Great Wall is nothing more than a prop constructed for a Hollywood blockbuster. Where is its aura of an old warrior proudly exhibiting his wounds? There is nothing left of its venerability acquired over centuries. For the first time during this trip, she is not looking forward to the walk. It is without her usual enthusiasm that she sets out to follow Alan towards the entrance.

Further on, she attempts to stride past a long row of souvenir shops and small stalls with noisy hawkers eager to sell their knick-knacks. When one of them shouting 'Hello' dangles a T-shirt with a printed 'I climbed the Great Wall' in front of her face, she glares at him as if she wanted to punch him. People are shuffling around everywhere, on the parking area, at the entrance gate, all over the ramparts. Having to push through such crowds does not help to dispel her gloom. The tour brochure did not lie, the Great Wall is 'the number-one tourist attraction' for Chinese and Westerners alike, and Badaling is its busiest section.

After taking the group through an arched gateway to enter the Wall, Alan explains that it is preferable to walk on the southern section. It is longer, but less crowded than the famously popular northern section. The group sets out to climb the steps leading in that direction, and reaches a level stretch with crenellated brick parapets and paved with large stone slabs, crossing a narrow canal. Along the way, they have to negotiate a passage between two rows of buffet tables, elaborately decorated and staffed by elegant Chinese waiters; all colour-coordinated in purple except for the white hats of the chefs busy cooking at black stoves. Let us watch B's reaction in front of such sacrilege? Can she really be stopping now, camera in hand? We can imagine the title she has in mind for her picture of that jarring scene, 'The Great Wall taken over by vandals.'

When she rejoins the others, she is intrigued to find them all standing at the entrance of a large renovated watchtower, laughing, their cameras clicking. They are facing a black panel with the words 'The Great Wall East Mountain' in white letters, and a smaller panel with a triangular sign showing a man slipping down, and the words 'Don't Fall Down' below Chinese characters. No doubt back in Britain these pictures will be passed around many times as a charming example of Chinese wisdom.

Exploring a watchtower here is a new experience. Instead of walking at ground level through a half-ruined construction, she is able to access both floors easily and safely. Once inside, it is no great effort for her to imagine a garrison of thirty to fifty men living here with their food supplies and weapons. From their commanding position at the top, sentries could keep a lookout in four directions and, at the slightest sign of approaching enemies, alert others to rush to repel them.

As she stands within the walls of the tower, B's imagination takes her irresistibly to the virtual reality of the past. She feels sorry for the millions of builders and soldiers whose lives were sacrificed to achieve the massive but misjudged project of protecting the 'civilized' Chinese from the northern tribes they feared and despised as 'barbarians.' It did not work out that way. Those 'barbarian' nomads found ways to bypass the Great Wall. Yet now, 'barbarian' tourists are neither able to avoid nor bypass the Great Wall at Badaling. She can choose to look at either side of the coin: the futile waste of human lives in the past, or what that grand construction is achieving today. Both are part of the astonishing story of the Great Wall. B comes out of the watchtower reconciled with the world.

Alan explains that for the first time they will reach an altitude of one thousand metres on this southern side, just as they would have done on the northern one. The prospect of reaching the Promised Land could not make B more blissfully happy.

For a while, the rise is gentle and takes them to a small platform. Decorated with red ribbons is a black statue of the

Buddha attaining enlightenment while seated under the Bohdi Tree. Further on, they arrive at the bottom of a long flight of steps leading to the first watchtower, called the South Fourth Tower. No need here to pick their way over rubble, to tiptoe on unstable stones, to scramble over crumbling steps, it is all newly repaired and looking perfectly safe. The shiny metal handrails running along each side of the Wall seem incongruous. B is ready to scamper to the top, but Emma insists on taking the group through the familiar stretching and warm-up routine before letting them begin the ascent.

Nothing they have climbed on the Great Wall until now is steeper than the gradient that they are facing.

'Why did you choose the southern side, Alan?' laments someone.

'Have you seen the other side, packed with people?' replies Alan, slightly vexed that his judgement is being questioned.

'At least they'll save some energy, they won't arrive at the top half-dead.'

'They'll reach the top as exhausted as you'll be. It gets very steep close to the summit before their last tower. But the view is amazing from both sides, I promise you.'

'Listen, everybody, have a Kit-Kat,' interrupts B. 'You can climb any gradient as long as you don't walk straight but zigzag up, and if you don't waste your breath talking.'

To suit the action to her words, she passes around a small bag of chocolate biscuits, slings her backpack over her shoulder, breathes deeply and launches into the ascent. Steps are cut into the nearly vertical incline at knee height, or in fact almost hip-high for B's short legs. As she feared, she needs to lift her bent knee up to her chest for her foot to reach the first step, but her trouser leg will not stretch enough to allow that. She recalls her adolescent despair when comparing herself with the leggy models in fashion magazines. But looking up at the seemingly endless flight of steps, going way up into the sky, acts as a wake-up call. It is her last day on the Great Wall. She must enjoy every minute. And every minute she will enjoy.

For the next half-hour she heaves herself up, she huffs and puffs, she gasps, she pants, but she never pauses nor grabs the handrail. What a salutary lesson in humility for her to find that her struggle has taken so long that she is the last to arrive at the top. For the first time, she has no choice but to collapse on the ground in front of the others, struggling to catch her breath. She has no qualms about doing so.

As always, Alan shows no sign of having made any effort to climb that stretch. Watching him makes B envious of the way he takes it all as if strolling along a country lane. He reminds her of the heroic generations of conscripted labourers who toiled to build the Great Wall, carrying heavy stones and bricks to dizzying heights, often along razor-edged ridges. How they must have dreamt at times of an intervention by a saviour like the poet Amphion, whose magical lyre caused the stones to build the walls of Thebes by themselves.

After a while, everyone gets up, ready to set out. They are confident that the toughest part of the climb is behind them. There are only gentle undulations between the last six towers before reaching the summit. Wisely, B refrains from pointing out to them that descending this steep section on the way back will be arduous and even dangerous. There may be little risk of tumbling when you climb up, but it is quite the opposite when you return. Some people may choose to descend backwards, facing the steps and holding on to the handrail.

'Before we start,' says Alan with a mischievous grin, 'I must quote Chairman Mao to you. I should have done it when you grumbled earlier, "He who does not reach the Great Wall is not a true man; and he who does not love the Great Wall is not a hero".'

'So, Mao was a misogynist as well as a tyrant. How about true women?' explodes the arch-feminist of the group.

'Whatever Mao says,' adds B with conviction, 'I love the Great Wall, but I'll never consider myself a hero to have reached it. In fact, I feel immensely privileged to walk on it.' This journey on the Great Wall is a unique chance that life has given her, and she has enjoyed every minute of it. She has no reason to feel proud.

The last section is an easy tower-to-tower walk, with a few short moderately steep ramps. There is plenty of time to admire the northern section of the Great Wall on the opposite hillside snaking up steep rolling mountains, with the Eighth North Tower dominating the highest point. In the narrow valley below, the tourists look like a toy army preparing to storm the Great Wall.

Suddenly there is a rumbling noise.

'Oh, here comes the train from Beijing,' explains Alan, 'Can you see it? It's the first railway line built by the Chinese a hundred years ago. And we've also arrived at our destination, the last South Tower of the reconstructed Badaling Great Wall. Now we turn around and retrace our steps.'

'Wait,' interrupts Emma, 'before we go back, let's use the steps of the ramp for the charity group photo.'

She extracts from her bulky rucksack a stock of NewShores

Children's Hospice T-shirts and distributes them. Alan takes a couple of pictures with Emma's camera, and is asked to repeat the operation with everyone else's camera. Afterwards, it starts all over again, but this time Alan joins the group facing the camera, and Emma takes on the role of official photographer. It could last for ever. B sits through it all smiling blissfully but her unseeing gaze is lost in the distance. She is not thinking about anything, just feeling; not even thinking about what she is feeling. It is her last chance to let all her senses absorb the essence of the Great Wall and store it in her heart where time cannot dissolve it.

Back on the valley floor, there is time to visit a small building, the Guan Yu temple. A panel at the entrance says that it is dedicated to a third-century general worshipped as a god. It was built in his memory in the mid-fifteenth century and completely rebuilt in 1997. Is there any fragment of the original in this perfect reconstruction, B wonders? Well, why not take a picture anyway? It will still look Chinese on glossy photo paper.

And how about the huge free-standing memorial arch next to it? With its three levels of upturned roof eaves on top of four tall red posts, and with the rich palette of colours of its intricate ornaments, it will make a splendid picture and impress friends at home. Yes, these are the down-to-earth thoughts that invade B's mind, pushing aside her earlier lofty philosophical reflections. After all, she is nothing more and nothing less than one of those anonymous tourists who shocked her when she arrived at Badaling.

When the time comes to board the coach, B slows down and stands motionless at its door. Her eyes follow the Great Wall clinging to the contours of the mountains, descending from the northern foothills to cross the pass and climbing up the southern side of the valley. She strives to store in her mind and heart vivid memories to last a lifetime. Nothing warned her to do that thirteen years ago when she dropped Eric at Heathrow for his year out. And a twenty-three-year-old son does not want you to take hundreds of pictures of him. Since then, she has grown wiser. Now, after trekking for days on a Great Wall that refuses to be anything but itself, that nothing can defeat, she has grown stronger. She believes that the life she had not bargained for is still a life where her son is himself and with her, a life that, come what may, is worth living.

Tonight she will dine on crispy Peking duck in a restaurant packed with tourists to celebrate the end and success of the charity challenge. And she will attend a spectacle of Chinese acrobatics, sitting in a theatre with an army of tourists. And she will sleep in a superb bedroom on the fortieth floor of the modern ZhongYan tourist hotel.

Tomorrow, she will be fascinated and thrilled to 'do' with Alan the Beijing traditional tourist sights selected by his superiors at the China National Tourism Administration: Tiananmen Square, the Forbidden City, a Silk Factory, a Fresh Water Pearl Shop. However dense the crowds of tourists surrounding her, she will still scribble frantically in her notebook and click manically her camera. But she will also imagine and share the silent stories that she can read in the multitude of expressive faces around her. She will be every one of these tourists; she will feel again part of the struggling but undefeated human race.

Why accuse her of unashamedly compromising her noble aspirations when she delights in the pleasures of being a regular tourist in Beijing? She deserves a memorable day touring that wonderful city, as much as anyone in the group. But we should leave her out of our story while she is enjoying herself without her friend the Great Wall. Let us meet her again tomorrow morning.

On the plane taking the group back to Britain, B is busy composing in her mind the letter of thanks that she will write to her sponsors. She wants them to know that she walked every kilometre of the trek, that it was an exciting and rewarding time. What is the best way to tell them how enjoyable it was? How about a list of what those ten days in China have brought her? That's easier said than done. When she mentions her problem to the others, they all want to join in. Soon they exchange ideas. They turn it into a competition, calling across the aisles over the heads of the puzzled passengers. Someone suggests drawing up a list in alphabetical order. They come up with a range of propositions from pertinent to far-fetched. 'Amazing scenery,' 'Breathtaking views,' 'Colourful villages,' 'Difficult passages.' It becomes harder work with 'X', 'Y', and 'Z', but no one wants to give up.

Rising to such an intellectual level, while breathing the re-circulated air of an airplane, is exhausting. Despite her efforts to be part of the general conversation that follows, B feels her eyes closing. In a few minutes, she loses consciousness. All her life, on cars, trains, or planes, she has been able to fall asleep almost on demand, and for the entire trip. Hours later, when she disembarks in Moscow, she sleepwalks through the transit enclosure. Back on the plane for the second leg of the flight, she has no difficulty dozing off again. The request to buckle seatbelts to prepare for landing at Heathrow wakes her up. She finds herself back in the world again, ready for new walks.

11½   Reflections

Our last walk today, GM. I don't want to think about it. I'll miss my Great Wall so much. I imagine already the withdrawal symptoms I'll endure tomorrow strapped in my seat on the plane. But enough of that, GM, I want to pause and reflect with you.

During these last ten days, you've had to listen to my questions, you've had to put up with my bouts of mistrust, of anger, of despair. How I admire you for remaining steadfastly by my side, for never giving up on me. You deserve a medal, and it's time I apologised for my behaviour and expressed my gratitude.

Looking back, I remember that I couldn't explain what urged me one day to go to China. Why did I feel that it was something I was right to do, that I had to do? It wasn't that I was seeking to evade the reality of Eric's death with which I am fated to live. I'm stranded on the lonely bank of a river from which there is no return. For me the bridge is broken beyond repair. Often the waters flow so furiously that it becomes impossible to be heard from one side to the other.

As a mother, GM, I'll always want the best to happen, not so much for myself, but for my children, whether alive or not. That desire will never let go of me. It will at times be crushingly oppressive. In moments of joy and achievement, I instinctively think of Eric's earthly existence cut short before he had his fair share of them, and I have to struggle to free myself from a tangle of contradictory emotions.

I'd like to believe that it's you, GM, who lured me to China. What a risk you took! Why? To what end? You knew what an exhilarating time I would have as a keen mountaineer climbing for days on that magnificent Great Wall. And you knew the intense pain it would stir up in me to find myself enjoying such a treat at my age when it is for ever refused to Eric.

And indeed, I went through a Hell of regrets on Heaven's Ladder. And a day later, simultaneously exalted by the glorious landscape of rugged mountains crested by the Jinshanling Wall, and shattered by the voice within me calling from the past, I literally collapsed. Each time, you gave Eric back to me, GM. He was there helping me to get up again, and to emerge from despair unharmed and stronger. Yes, afterwards I was in a daze, but still able to resume the walk and to enjoy the climb.

Such intense experiences speak louder than words. They tell me, GM, that you don't need to explain to me, to argue with me, to prove to me. You have other ways of saying everything about the essential. How could I fail to listen to you, just as you intend me to? Why did I reproach you for remaining silent? I'm sorry to have railed against you and pestered you for answers. I see now that my questions are pointless. How astute of you, GM, to wait patiently until at last I'm able to hear the answers I need. I truly admire your subtle ways with me.

You wanted me to grow through the ordeal of missing Eric more than ever, as I did during that journey on the Great Wall, and you knew it would happen. It was a harsh and risky treatment, but it worked. It made me feel with all my being how resilient I am. From now on, whenever I struggle and long again to reach across the divide, I know that I can count on your support. There will be more moments in my life when, announced or not, the past will erupt into the present and throw me off balance. But I'll find the strength to steady myself and keep walking, and when I fail, you and Eric will be there to pick me up and set me on the path again. I'm confident that you will both be at my side to reassure me, and to show me the way to welcome life again.

Why did I fail to understand what you'd planned for me, GM? Why did I take so long to decipher correctly the clues you planted on my path? Sometimes you're too subtle for me. You know me and I'm sure you're prepared to wait patiently until I'm receptive to the plans you have in store for me. And sure enough, today, at last, I'm able to shine the right light on what has happened to me. Everything becomes clear and falls into place.

Let me remind you, GM, of those remarkable events and how they have given a sense to my life. Four months ago, by what I thought was chance, I glimpsed a leaflet about a charity walk to raise money for a children's hospice. I ignored it for two weeks but suddenly found myself one morning deciding to join it. Raising funds was hard work for a novice like me. Strangely, it felt as if I had no choice but to obey a mysterious call, and at the same time I found it a most satisfying assignment. To my amazement, extraordinary rewards followed. The offer of half my middle granddaughter's fortune moved me to tears, while the response of my many generous donors exceeded my wildest dreams and filled me with gratitude and intense joy.

Then a chain of unexpected mishaps could easily have turned the whole expedition into a disaster. Recurrent cellulitis only days before departure could have forced me to stay at home. Next, airport security declared our plane unfit to fly to China and a whole day of the challenge was wasted, ironically at Heathrow's Best Western Hotel. During the flight, a locker opened above me and I received six bottles of vodka on my head. What else could go wrong?

After all that, when I reached China, who would have thought that I'd be instantly overwhelmed on my first contact with the Great Wall. That awe-inspiring structure exudes an intensity of presence that no words can properly describe, and nothing had prepared me to feel an immediate affinity between its story and mine. It cast a spell on me that will never be broken.

Day after day, GM, it lent me its ramparts in the grand setting of the YanShan mountains. I had no need to know where I was going or why. I was never forced to turn around, or to choose between directions. It guided me. I had only to stride ahead. Walking gave free rein to my thoughts, let my imagination run wild. In my mind, I travelled in the distant Chinese past, and I travelled in my own ephemeral past on its trail of memories. It was a unique chance and a privilege to dedicate those ten days to celebrating Eric's life.

For thirteen years, I have been torn apart by pain, a pain that is now part of me for ever. The Great Wall has been torn apart for millennia by wars, by ideologies, and today by consumerism. We are both damaged. And yet, we both still find the strength to climb along rocky precipices, and to plunge into deep ravines. No slope is too steep for us, no crumbling steps can stop us.

GM, it was exhilarating to walk with you and Eric. I see now that you were in charge from the moment I said, 'I am going to China'. You knew that no slow sedate climb would give me the full measure of my resilience. You decided that trekking on the Great Wall would do so, and it did. Thanks to your wise choice, I am now aware of my inner strength, and I am confident that it can only increase over the years. Pain does not go away, but thanks to you, and with Eric's help, I shall always defeat it whenever it strikes.

During that wonderful journey I learnt to apply new criteria to my life that no logic can destroy or penetrate. I acquired knowledge that 'transcends all understanding.' The death of a child calls the whole universe into question for grieving parents, but a question without an answer in this world. On the day I succumbed to grief and hit bottom, you were there to rescue me. You took me to a world where the words 'No more', 'Never again', 'If only', were replaced by a voice whispering, 'He is still Here'. At that moment, I felt intimations of timelessness, I sensed a hidden meaning. Suffering led to exhilarating and everlasting joy.

GM, you made this trek a beautiful and unique adventure for me, one that I'll never forget. Thank you.

Part Three

HOMECOMING

12

B's story goes on

Inside Heathrow airport, the security personnel watching the CCTV must be wondering whether B is smuggling some illegal substance. They must have noticed her blatantly jumping the queue at passport control, and pushing people aside to grab her suitcase on the carousel. She smiles an innocent smile as she walks casually past customs officers checking the luggage of younger-looking passengers, and then turns into the exit corridor. Now, she runs so fast that the automatic door hardly has time to open and she almost crashes into it.

On the other side, she searches for her husband in the crowd of people who are trying to attract the attention of arriving loved ones or business colleagues. Exhilaration surges up inside her when she spots him. During the trek, she has kept her home life with its memories on hold. Today, for the first time since she left him at the departure hall ten days ago, she allows herself to be aware that she missed him in China. Not terribly, of course, there was too much to occupy her mind. But here, when they embrace, the emotions jostling to manifest themselves are too intense to translate immediately into a deep or even sensible exchange. 'Are you well?' she asks, and at the same time she hears him saying, 'How was it in China?' But they both know that an old married couple does not need big words and long sentences to express the vital signs of their relationship.

Before they leave the terminal, they wait for all the members of the NewShores group to come out of the restricted area. When Jimmy, the Indian tour doctor appears, three generations of his family rush to embrace him tearfully, as if he were a hostage returning after years of captivity. Glancing at B out of the corner of his eye, he flashes a smile at her while raising his eyebrows and shrugging imperceptibly. He knows that she is struggling to banish memories of waiting for Eric, and rushing to embrace him when he came through that door. A hugging session is just beginning before the group takes leave of each other, and she joins in. Firm promises to keep in touch, to get together regularly, are exchanged. Undertaking any challenge creates an esprit de corps and B feels it, despite having distanced herself during the trek.

As they drive home in the heavy morning traffic, her husband tries hard to follow the description of each day in the torrent of details that she is pouring out excitedly. When they arrive, she keeps talking while he opens the door, carries her suitcase upstairs, and makes her sit down with a cup of coffee. Even the telephone call that he hurries to answer does not silence her. When he hangs up and turns towards her, he raises both hands, as if to defend himself against an assailant, and explains apologetically, 'I am so sorry to stop you, but I've got to go. The meeting I should be chairing has started and everybody is waiting for me. I've really got to go. I'd much rather hear about your trip, but we'll catch up this afternoon.'

Such a familiar episode convinces her that she is definitely back at home. She cannot resist replying, 'Don't worry, I've not forgotten how busy you are.' Does she want him to feel slightly guilty? Why not just smile angelically and say that she needs some time alone to collect her thoughts. She wants to present them in a way that does justice to what the trip has brought into her life. How can she share the ineffable?

After waving goodbye, she goes to her study and closes the door. She needs to retreat into herself, to find a respite. As ever, music offers her a refuge. An irrepressible desire to immerse herself in it seizes her. She selects Schubert's Quintet, Opus 163. Will she still hear in it a soothing voice that uses no words, as she has done so many times in the past? Will its ebb and flow rock her once again, wash through her like a tide, free her mind of debris?

As soon as she switches on her CD player, Schubert's music, a music that is not of this world, irradiates her and transports her back to the Great Wall, opening her up to the intangible forces that carry us through life. The aching lament of the sublime adagio floods her with unbearable sorrow before lifting her irresistibly into the serene pastures beyond grief. This music encompasses all human life but also transcends it. It spreads pure happiness within her. Schubert's celestial world speaks to her deepest self, and makes her lose all desire to ask questions, all craving for answers. In that shelter, her tormented soul is overcome by a feeling of bliss that effaces heartache. Pain is transformed into tranquil joy.

After the music stops, she sits motionless for a while, weeping silently from the turmoil and exaltation she has experienced. She turns towards the framed picture standing on the corner of her desk, smiles at it and murmurs, '*Merci*, Eric.'

Now she is ready to meet the world. People will want to draw up for her the balance sheet at the end of her trek on the Great Wall. They will want her to have gained 'peace,' they will mention 'catharsis,' 'closure.' They want her to 'move on.' It would reassure them, calm their own existential fears. But how could she find comfort in such a pretence? They are kind and mean well, but she does not make sense to them. They are happily sharing their news with all of their children living close by or somewhere in the world, they are still rejoicing or worrying for all of them, they are still laughing or crying with all of them. Can she or her husband do the same? No. Can their daughter talk to her brother about her children, about her life as a GP? No.

To tell others the true story of the last two weeks, she has to describe the extraordinary events of her journey that make her feel that Eric is at her side, protecting her, guiding her, enriching her life in varied and unexpected ways, as he did when he was alive. She has to convince them that these precious moments fill her personal treasure chest with invisible riches, that she knows there are more to come. She has to persuade them that the joy of feeling the presence of her son in her life lights a fire in the cold recesses of her soul where she is grieving for him. No longer is her life a life without Eric.

Will she find the right way to reject admiring comments about her intrepidity in tackling the challenge of the trek? It is difficult to be taken as truthful when you proclaim loudly that you do not deserve to be praised. Will she be able to change the views of the uninitiated? They see such a trek as a torment.

They refuse to see it as the exhilarating physical pleasure it was for her.

The word 'challenge' will pop up. Does it apply to her adventure in the way they expect it does? Did not hiking for days on the Great Wall require from her endurance and a youthful attitude? Of course it did. Above all, they must accept that it actually refuelled her with energy. But will she be able to explain that at times it was unbearable to her to benefit from such strength at her age, an age that Eric will never reach? How can she explain that she often had to battle against memories that drained her of her very substance and left her unable to walk on?

Yes, to meet that challenge she often had to summon up her courage, superhuman courage even, when despair stood in the way, when the excruciating reality of Eric's death confronted her. She panicked, she struggled, and she had to brace herself to face her suffering. In the end, she had triumphed. And she realised then that, when life puts her resilience to the test, she is not alone, Eric is still there.

There is no public recognition for accepting to forge ahead with one's destiny, for discovering new resolve in oneself, but privately she tells herself that on the Great Wall of China she deserved a personal badge of courage.

By the time her husband returns, she has regained her composure. She remembers at last to enquire with great interest about his various activities while she was away. He has evidently been able to survive without her. During a surreptitious tour of the house, she has been amazed to find the refrigerator full, no dirty dishes in the sink, clean towels on the bathroom rails. He interrupts her questions, begging her to resume the account of her adventures where she had broken off earlier.

So much to report. For hours she attempts to describe the Great Wall and the impact it had on her. She shows him the beautifully decorated China National Tourism Certificate saying 'Did climb the Great Wall' that Alan gave her. She re-enacts her amusing encounters with the locals. She demonstrates how she used a zip wire and a toboggan at the end of her walks. Neither would like her to shorten her recital. She talks as if she is still walking in those YanShan mountains. He savours journeying with her.

Before the day ends, why not eavesdrop on the last words they exchange as they are drifting off to sleep?

'I am so happy that you enjoyed this trip.'

'Yes, it was an extraordinary time. I'll write a book about it.'

Acknowledgements

Thoughts about this book have been in my mind for nearly a decade, but have been slow to become a travel memoir. I am immensely grateful to all the people who put up with my constant bragging that I would finish it some day.

First and foremost, my thanks go to my everlastingly English husband who during the book's gestation and production has had the mental strength to accept and deal with my increasingly frequent Gallic outbursts of despair or exasperation.

Special thanks are due to my daughter, Isabelle, for her continuing support, and to my sister, Muriel, for her generous comments and her expertise.

I want to record my thanks to Dr Clare Morgan, Dr Sarah Burton and the late Nick Kneale for their invaluable advice and unfailing encouragement. I have greatly benefited from a workshop and lectures in Professor Dame Hermione Lee's Oxford Centre for Life-Writing.

The positive comments of the literary agent, Catherine Clarke, stimulated me to complete the book. I am grateful to Sarah Juckes of Completely Novel for helping me to publish it. A special mention is due to the talented and sensitive Henry Rivers who designed a book cover expressing perfectly what is at the core of my book.

I am deeply indebted to the many friends who read parts of the manuscript, and whose generous comments made me persevere: Adrian, Charles, Jane, Jenny, John, Marilyn, Mungo, Robert, Therese and Yvonne, to name but a few.

The book would not have been the same had I not had the chance to walk with Alan, an outstanding Great Wall tour guide and a wonderful human being.

Above all I want to express my eternal gratitude to **Eric**. But for the gift of his life, this book would never have been written.